The Last Normal Child

Recent Titles in
Childhood in America
Sharna Olfman, Series Editor

All Work and No Play . . . : How Educational Reforms
Are Harming Our Preschoolers
Sharna Olfman, editor

Childhood Lost: How American Culture Is Failing Our Kids
Sharna Olfman, editor

No Child Left Different
Sharna Olfman, editor

The Last Normal Child

Essays on the Intersection of Kids, Culture, and Psychiatric Drugs

LAWRENCE H. DILLER, M.D.

Childhood in America
Sharna Olfman, Series Editor

Westport, Connecticut
London

Library of Congress Cataloging-in-Publication Data

Diller, Lawrence H.
　　The last normal child : essays on the intersection of kids,
　culture, and psychiatric drugs / Lawrence H. Diller.
　　　　p.　cm. — (Childhood in America)
　　Includes bibliographical references and index.
　　ISBN 0–275–99096–6 (alk. paper)
　　1. Psychotropic drugs. 2. Children—Drug use.
　3. Culture—Social aspects. I. Title.
　　RM315.D5522　2006
　　615'.788083—dc22　　　　2006021003

British Library Cataloguing in Publication Data is available.

Library of Congress Catalog Card Number: 2006021003
ISBN: 0–275–99096–6

First published in 2006

Praeger Publishers, 88 Post Road West, Westport, CT 06881
An imprint of Greenwood Publishing Group, Inc.
www.praeger.com

Printed in the United States of America

The paper used in this book complies with the
Permanent Paper Standard issued by the National
Information Standards Organization (Z39.48–1984).

10　9　8　7　6　5　4　3　2

To the memory of Sandra Brand,
my family's first author

Contents

Acknowledgments

"Fun" is not a word I would ever choose to describe writing this or any book. Writing a book is simply too much work to be described as fun. However, writing *The Last Normal Child* has been a mostly pleasurable experience because I think it is the most personal and candid of the three books I've written thus far. Part of this pleasure has come from the continuing support and interaction I've had from both colleagues and friends in writing these essays over a six-year period.

Russell Barkley has repeatedly offered me time to discuss ideas, theories, and concerns about ADHD and medication. He is one of the few researchers and theorists in this field who is willing to enter the realm of ethics and politics in his statements and writings. Wayne Camara of the Educational Testing Service, which administers the SAT, also was very generous with his time on the telephone with me. I also very much want to thank others who consented to interviews for these essays: Nadine Lambert, Stephen Hinshaw, William Pelham, William Carey, Laurence Greenhill, Dolores Sargent, and Eric Myers.

Sam Goldstein and I collaborated on one of the essays in this book, and I greatly appreciate his continuing efforts to "make me respectable" within the academic elite circles of ADHD research and professional publications. Rich Simon, editor and publisher of the *Psychotherapy Networker*, has now for two decades published my work and has been a continued support for my ideas and efforts. Similarly, Karen Croft at *Salon.com* was highly receptive and supportive of my writing in that online magazine for three years.

I thank Sharna Olfman, the series editor for Praeger's Childhood in America series, and Debbie Carvalko, the editor at Praeger, for their interest and support in this project. Every writer benefits from rewrites, and Leigh Ann Hirschman, Susan Tasaki, and Mary Sykes-Wylie have wonderfully cleaned up some of my prose in these essays. My agent, Beth Vesel, continues to be a steadfast support and believer in my writing and larger concerns.

Others who have helped in conversation and friendship through the years include Peter Kramer, David Healy, William Carey, Julie Zito, Erik Parens, Gretchen LeFever, Glen Elliott, Jack Obedzinki, Sue Parry, Jon Weil, Sabina Morganti, Mary-Jane Nunes-Temple, Vivian Diller, and John Jacobs. My wife, Denise, remains an invaluable source of feedback, support, and grounding when I get either too excited or boring about these subjects. My sons, Martin and Louie, now both in their late teenage years, have provided me a forum to express ideas to a generation most affected by the changes in diagnosis and treatment of children's emotional and performance problems. Their perspective is unique and infiltrates much of the writing of this book.

Finally, this book is dedicated to my recently deceased aunt, Sandra Brand, my mother's older sister. As my mother's mental faculties declined, Sandra, who lived to the age of ninety-six, remained quite sharp. In our weekly telephone calls, her deep interest in and caring about my writing and broad concerns for children in America soothed me as I faced the loss of my mother's abilities. Sandra also wrote books, and her delight at my successes could only come from a mother or surrogate. She will be missed.

The essays in this collection, most of which have never been published before, are organized into three parts and a postscript. All previously published essays have been revised and updated. The first part addresses the influence of science, politics, money, and culture on the diagnosis and treatment of children's emotional problems in the United States. The middle raises specific situations in which children's behavior, family actions, and psychiatric drugs intersect in America today. The third part analyzes the "industry"— drug companies and academic medicine—and the effect their efforts have on the way we view and treat children's behavior and their problems in this country. The postscript is a reflection on more personal factors in my professional and private life that have influenced my thinking and practice as a doctor.

Part I

The Influence of Science, Politics, Money, and Culture on Psychiatric Diagnosis and Treatment of Children in America

1

The Last Normal Child:
America's Intolerance
of Diversity in Children's
Performance and Behavior

If you're old enough, you remember Professor Ned Brainard, the character originated by famous film and TV actor Fred MacMurray in the eponymous Disney film of 1962, *The Absent-Minded Professor*. Poor Ned could never find his keys. He'd leave machines running in his laboratory. He kept his family waiting forever. He even forgot to show up for his own wedding. Brainard was obsessed with discovering Flubber, an antigravity substance that would allow the players on his college's basketball team to leap over the hoop (and this was long before the movie *White Men Can't Jump*).

MacMurray (perhaps most famous for his role as the father in the long-running television series *My Three Sons*) played Brainard with a sweet, inoffensive nature. He meant to hurt no one and was genuinely sorry when his lapses caused problems. Audiences found this apologetic bumbling genius so appealing that the Walt Disney company produced a Flubber sequel featuring MacMurray's lovable character with all his faults. As a testament to the character's enduring appeal, in 1997 Robin Williams appeared as the absent-minded professor in a remake called *Flubber*.

Yet times do change. For the families with children in today's America, the appeal of an absent-minded professor elicits far less appreciation. I actually just medicated Ned with Ritalin. The Ned I'm referring to is the pseudonym I've given an eight-year-old child who came with his parents to see me in my capacity as a behavioral/developmental pediatrician.

This Ned hadn't been performing up to his abilities in his third-grade class. He attended a prestigious local private school in my area, an upper-middle–class suburb of the San Francisco Bay area. Ned seemed pretty miserable over his C grades. This wasn't failing, but his parents and the school expected so much more from Ned. It didn't help that both his parents had finished graduate school, and Ned's IQ had tested out at 130. Ned's mood in my office ranged from thoughtful to depressingly somber and reflected the collective disappointment over his performance.

But I saw Ned Brainard in this child. My Ned was a bespectacled mild-mannered introvert who loved to read. I never saw him without a book in his hand. This eight-year-old had read each of the Harry Potter books in his spare time, including the then most recent 870-page *Harry Potter and the Order of the Phoenix*. But he had trouble getting his homework done. When Ned sat down at the kitchen table to complete his assignments, his mind and body would drift away to subjects that were of more interest to him than his math (for which he demonstrated an aptitude) and Spanish (yes, in the third grade).

"Right at the moment, I'm really into the Sahara, Doctor Diller," he told me. He was finishing a high school-level adventure book that took place in the desert. He'd also begun a book his mother had bought him, an adult-level nonfiction work on the Sahara region. And Ned had downloaded more information about deserts in general from the Internet. Kristy, his mother, despite her concerns and frustrations over Ned's school performance, could appreciate and support her child's intelligence and broad range of interests. But why, she complained to me in front of Ned and her husband, Harold, couldn't he just get his homework turned in on time?

Also, she said he seemed less able to focus in the classroom and appeared to daydream during instruction time. He was not a behavior problem for his teacher. He wasn't disruptive or a bother to the other kids. Though not the most popular or a class leader, he was well liked and even respected for "being brainy." But his teacher, Mrs. Gill, was very frustrated.

Mrs. Gill also had trouble getting Ned to turn in his class work or homework on a timely basis. She was hesitant to punish Ned for unfinished class work or for his missed or late assignments. "He's such a nice boy," the teacher had said to Kristy when explaining why she declined to hold him from recess or keep him after school. Instead she would give him a zero for his failure to timely complete the tasks that were assigned. It was only Ned's excellent performance on tests that kept his grades at the C level. Obviously Ned was learning all the material, but he was not conforming to the school's standards for excellence.

Kristy was at her wit's end. She was the parent assigned in the family to monitor the school and homework. Everything Kristy tried to do—constant verbal reminders to get the homework done, sitting next to him as he worked, providing rewards and punishments, checking his backpack every day before he left for school to make certain his assignments were there—still failed to get Ned organized and efficient. Homework that should have taken about an hour would consume the entire afternoon and evening (with a break only for dinner). Ned somehow still "forgot" to turn his homework in when Mrs. Gill asked for it. Kristy would at times lose her cool and scream at Ned when she would discover the work from the day before still in his binder. Ned felt embarrassed and sad. He was at a loss to explain his behavior except to say he might have been reading when Mrs. Gill asked for the work.

Ned's parents (Ned's father, Harold, who usually only came home around 7 PM from his investment brokerage company, canceled his work engagements to attend this afternoon meeting) wanted to know if Ned had attention-deficit/hyperactivity disorder (ADHD). Ned clearly wasn't hyperactive, his parents acknowledged, but they wondered whether his problems of attention and organization were beyond his control. Perhaps his problems were the result of a brain problem, they speculated. Maybe he needed Ritalin.

As I got to know Ned and his world, Ned hardly struck me as a boy with a brain disease or psychiatric disorder. He was pleasant. He was smart. He was interesting. Yes, in the classroom he was performing below the expectations for his high IQ. Still, he was clearly learning—just not demonstrating it to his teacher in the prescribed fashion of classroom participation and homework.

I first attempted to help Ned's parents and teacher change Ned's behavior with nondrug interventions. In particular I wanted Kristy to stop sitting by Ned and verbally keeping him on task during his homework. We agreed that she would set him up with his work and then set a timer for twenty-minute intervals. If he completed the section in time, she'd place a dollar sign in a checkbook ledger, which represented fifty cents. Ned could use this money to buy actual items or toys, but we also established that he could spend this money to "purchase" time on the weekends with his father in an activity of his choice. If he failed to complete sufficient work for each interval, he would lose fifteen minutes of reading time that night.

I hoped to successfully motivate Ned by using rewards and punishments that were immediately meaningful to him. Ned did care about the consequences of his poor grades, but I hypothesized that they were too delayed and too abstract to have much effect every afternoon when he sat down to do his work. I also wanted to decrease his dependency on his mother's constant (albeit quite inefficient) reinforcement when she sat next to him while he worked at his assignments.

Mrs. Gill was to try a similar strategy, assigning him dollar signs in class for similar short intervals of fifteen or twenty minutes spent successfully completing his work. If he performed poorly during this highlighted time of "dollar opportunities," his participation in the next pleasurable activity, such as recess or computers, could be delayed by five minutes after the rest of the students started.

This plan sounded good in the office, but after two months not much progress had been made. I could have guessed. Mrs. Gill wasn't particularly enthusiastic about the use of external reinforcers. She was a strong believer that motivation should come from within. Ironically she seemed to have already made up her mind that Ned "was ADHD," based upon her experience seeing other children in her class "turn it around" when they started taking Ritalin. It seemed, according to Kristy and Ned, that she had tried the dollar-opportunities approach only a couple of times.

It was harder to tell what exactly was happening at home over the two months. Ned did earn some money and lose some reading time, but overall he and his mother hadn't changed their pattern all that much. I suspected that Kristy found it hard to be consistent every day, especially when Ned had baseball practice or chess team (it was no surprise that he was the best chess player in his elementary school). On those days, they wouldn't get home until 6 PM, and by then Kristy would have to get dinner ready for her family, and Ned was on his own.

But I also sensed that Kristy in general didn't like getting tough with her sensitive son until his failures exasperated her. Then she would blow her cool and promise severe punishments but not follow through on the consequences once she had settled down. I also tried to get Harold more involved with his son, especially in supervising some of the homework completion. Harold made promises to his wife and son about coming home sooner and agreed to 5:30 PM, but his arrival time usually turned out closer to 7 PM. Kristy felt like too much of a failure in her "assigned" role as primary parent to protest too much about Harold's perpetual tardiness. Now they were both back in my office with their son maintaining that Ned was ADHD and should try Ritalin.

I was in a quandary. I tried my best to get Ned's parents and teacher to make changes I thought would help. I knew that Ned's parents, though they appreciated his intelligence and gentle personality, worried about Ned losing ground in school and were even more concerned that Ned's mood, self-image, and self-esteem were suffering. Might he not do better and feel better if he were taking a drug that improved his focus and organization?

This scene could take place only in the United States. We use 80 percent of the world's Ritalin.[1] Ours is the only country in the world where the "symptoms" of forgetfulness, dreaminess, and intelligence—in short, the characteristics of the absent-minded professor or child—would be considered signs of a mental disorder to be treated with a psychiatric drug. I, in my role as a specialist, do this all the time—medicate children with drugs like Ritalin, Adderall, and Prozac, much more frequently than I care to—even when I feel they have *nothing seriously wrong with them*. Ned and many of the kids I medicate are normal children. How can I justify doing this? How did this situation come to be?

There have always been problem children. Every society has a way of explaining these kids and managing them. The concept of childhood became widespread in Western Europe only about three hundred years ago. Before then, children, when considered at all, were thought of as small adults. For about two hundred years, Western culture believed that religious or spiritual deficiencies were responsible for children's misbehavior or poor learning. Prayer and physical punishments were the remedies for these ills.

Freud's ideas first swept Europe one hundred years ago and by the 1920s had become the predominant theoretical framework for understanding and treating children's problems in America. Freud's popularity was limited primarily to the professional class of doctors, teachers, and wealthy families. By the 1950s Freud's ideas had trickled down to the middle class but were never fully accepted. Most Americans still viewed their kids' problems as signs of laziness or moral weakness. Treatment in mainstream America was far more likely to be a spanking than an hour in play therapy with a child analyst.

Boiled down, Freudian theory posits that all children's problems are the results of unresolved internal conflict caused by stress in their relationships with their mothers. The pediatrician Benjamin Spock was the great popularizer of Freudian notions through his books on

child care and raising.[2] Compared with previous advice and guidance, Spock's message to parents was to relax and be more tolerant of
their children's needs and wants (which often was critically interpreted as a push towards permissiveness). This was the reigning ide-
ology for psychiatrists and pediatricians when I was in medical school
and residency between 1972 and 1978. Treatment for children's problems, when treatment was undertaken, was play therapy. But a revolution was taking place in psychiatry. That news broke through to me
and attracted the public's attention with the publication of the third
edition of the *Diagnostic and Statistical Manual* (*DSM-III*) in 1980.[3]

The *DSM* is America's psychiatric bible. It is the official arbiter
between normalcy and disorder according to the medical and psychiatric establishment—no matter that most of the categories of disorders
in this and subsequent versions of the *DSM* (since 1980 there have
been two more versions, the latest being *DSM-IV-TR*[4]) are not based
on any scientific data but on panels of experts' opinion. The *DSM* is
also critical because it becomes the basis for getting health services or
financial reimbursement for the patient or the doctor. In the end, the
bureaucratic and financial utility of the *DSM* likely trumps its scientific value—but of course that would be strongly challenged by the
psychiatric establishment.

Whatever its validity, the *DSM-III* was a radical departure from
the previous sixty years of Freudian thinking about behavior. Mother
was no longer blamed for Johnny's behavior. Neither was Johnny
himself to blame. Rather, Johnny's brain, as shaped by his genetics
and pedigree and controlled by his neural chemistry, was responsible
for Johnny's problems. Each discrete diagnosis implied that there was
a specific treatment, a drug, for each problem the child had.

When the *DSM-III* appeared in 1980, I initially approved. It
seemed an improvement over the abstruse and vague disorders of the
Freudian era. (Among the reasons for *DSM-III*'s radical break from
the previous version was the inability of doctors to agree upon diagnosis based upon *DSM-II*. Without agreement on diagnosis, research
on the disorders or their treatment was impossible. Psychiatry risked
being thrown out of academic medicine.) In the *DSM-III*, officially, the
diagnoses were descriptive only. They included lists of behavioral criteria that were technically etiologically neutral (no causes were
invoked). I saw it as an acceptable research tool. I never realized these
categories would become the ukases of clinical psychiatry.

Even in 1980 I already knew that children's problems were dimensional (over a range), not categorical (either you have it, or you don't),
the way they were defined in the *DSM-III*. I could ignore the *DSM-II*
because the categories were so vague. Quickly, however, the *DSM-III*

became the defining tool of my profession—precisely because it was well adapted for insurance companies and billing procedures. Suddenly, I couldn't ignore the *DSM-III*. I was not yet aware of a sub-rosa agenda by the leaders of psychiatry to ascribe biological causes to each specific disease entity that was described in the *DSM-III*.

This shift in focus from nurture to nature did not occur overnight. There were scientific murmurs challenging Freud as early as the 1950s, with studies examining inborn temperaments and personality traits of babies and toddlers.[5] Clinical improvements with drugs like Thorazine and lithium strongly suggested that behavior could change with a biological intervention (though then, as now, Freudians would claim the drugs only addressed the symptoms, not the fundamental cause of the bad behaviors).[6]

So the psychiatric world was changing slowly toward embracing a biological view of mental illness and health. Then the introduction of Prozac in 1988 changed everything. Prozac's target illness was major depression (a marketing, not clinical, decision[7]).[8] Clinical depression before Prozac's release was a rather infrequent psychiatric diagnosis in America. But as Prozac was introduced, Eli Lilly directed a major marketing, or educational, campaign at doctors. By the mid-1990s, depression had replaced anxiety as the most frequently diagnosed adult psychiatric disorder. Not only did Prozac change what condition ailed America the most, it also changed our very perspective of who did or did not have a true psychiatric disorder.

Peter Kramer's 1993 book *Listening to Prozac*[9] offered us his notion of "cosmetic psychopharmacology," and Kramer got it right. With fewer side effects than the older line of antidepressants, Prozac took off as a treatment for the walking emotionally wounded—people neither suicidal nor stuck in their beds, but those who didn't like their sensitivity or who wanted to feel "better than well." Rather than acting solely as a mood elevator, Prozac's nonspecific effect of improving emotional resiliency made it universally appealing for any sort of human emotional travail.

But because Prozac was a newly marketed prescription drug supposedly for depression, doctors began to diagnose this condition in everyone. Problems that had once been called anxiety, a general malaise called dysthymia, or some other vague mixed emotional state were now all "depression." It really didn't matter because Prozac "worked."

America's experience with Prozac led to an understandable but ultimately reductionistic illogical conclusion: If a pill (chemical) fixes the problem, then the problem must be caused by too little of that chemical. Aspirin fixes headaches, yet no one claims that headache sufferers have an "aspirin deficiency."[10] Still, "chemical imbalance" assumed preeminence in the minds of the public and doctors alike as an explanation for maladaptive behavior. And simplistic logic dictates that one treats a chemical imbalance with a pill.

I know all this seems a long way from Ned and me, but bear with me, and follow this genealogy. To use biblical parlance, Prozac use in adults begat Ritalin use in children, which begat use of Adderall, Concerta, and then Prozac and other psychiatric drugs in children. The use of each previous drug made the use of the next drug more acceptable and more frequent in children. By the mid-1990s, brain-based mental disorders and medications had become the accepted explanations and treatments for children's emotional, behavioral, and performance problems in America. So by the time I saw Ned in 2002, mainstream thinking said that his problems were also caused by some imbalance with his brain chemistry that should be treated with a pill.

The demands on children's educational performance and behavior in school have vastly increased over the past twenty-five years. I shake my head in uneasy wonderment when I compare what pediatricians considered "normal" development for a five-year-old in 1980 with pediatricians' performance expectations for five-year-olds today. Before 1990 I was satisfied with a child's intellectual growth (meaning I felt his development would pose no problem for him in his daily life) if at age five the child spoke clearly and used and understood oral language like other children his age. But I then became aware of a downward push, coming down from the high schools through middle and grade schools and affecting the goals of early childhood education. So by the early 1990s, five-year-olds were expected to decode letters and sounds, write and spell simple words, and perform simple addition and subtraction. These are skills that for decades had been taught to six-year-olds who were entering first grade but now were expected a year earlier at the kindergarten level. Please keep in mind that although twelve months may not seem like a long period of time, it represents 20 percent of a five-year-old's life.

The pressure to perform is so strong that it is present even during the toddler years. Preschools initially were developed to help inner-city impoverished youth become familiar and comfortable with the student–teacher relationships at an age before formal kindergarten education was mandated.[11] Now preschools prepare the children of the middle and upper-middle class for the rigors of kindergarten. For three- and four-year-olds, that means less time playing outside or using the indoor play kitchen and more "circle time" gathered around a teacher, having to sit still, focus, and learn pre-academic skills.

The rat race begins early for kids these days. They must get into and perform well in preschool in order to be ready for kindergarten. Elementary school prepares them for the infamous emotional gauntlet of middle school. Early high school readies them for late high school—"when it counts." And the number of advanced placement classes and extracurricular activities they take in high school give them a leg up in reaching the holy grail of secondary education—the "good" four-year college.

I'm getting tense and tired just writing about this. Imagine the pressures on children, families, and teachers who must live it. Depending upon a student's or family's economic class, ethnicity, and geographic area, a "good college" could be anything from a state school to one of the Ivy League or elite, smaller New England colleges. But attendance at a four-year college is considered an economic must. Anything less ostensibly dooms a child to an existence of low-paying jobs, which in America translates to consumer purgatory.

The loss of manufacturing jobs and outsourcing of services to the third world and the declining American standard of living (it requires two incomes per household in 2000 whereas one was sufficient in 1970) have sent shudders of anxiety all the way down to our education of two-year-olds. But the human brain, which took hundreds of thousands of years to evolve, cannot change over thirty years to adapt to our accelerated demands. Although many children are capable of handling the more difficult curriculum, a large minority cannot. Boys who struggle in school are often identified and labeled "deficient" in the preschool and elementary grades. The inadequate girls are often not discovered until middle or high school. Twenty years ago, most of these kids would have been considered developmentally normal. Now they are diagnosed with learning disorders because they cannot meet the new standards.

But they are often not noticed for their academic deficiencies. Instead many kids are given diagnoses of ADHD, oppositional behavior, anxiety, or depression as their behavior deteriorates under the stress. Boys typically act out or become overactive. Girls may daydream or become anxious. Many of the children who have difficulty with the tougher academic requirements show signs of mild to moderate depression. Ned defied the gender stereotype, and he didn't have a clear learning problem. Yet he wasn't "focusing" on his work. He too was caught in this same net of anxiety over performance at a very early age and was destined to be categorized as abnormal.

There's nothing inherently wrong with Ned or these other children. They have talents and personalities that come as round pegs, but they must fit one way or another into fairly rigid square educational holes.

Rather than looking closely at the fit and changing the hole (setting realistic expectations, incorporating special education, and supporting nonacademic talents, for example), we try to change the kid or lubricate the fit with a drug.

Once, before an audience, I debated another doctor over whether American children are overmedicated. He displayed a chart of income levels based on completion of high school, college, or graduate school to make the case that medication keeps children successful at school. The solutions for our stressed-out children are clear: Ritalin for focus and concentration beginning in preschool; Prozac for the emotional stress of high school and college. Depakote or Risperdal is reserved for those truly acting-out adolescents who haven't yet "found their place" (in other words, the square educational hole) in society.

The income argument for psychiatric medication is persuasive if one accepts the fundamental premise that money equals happiness. Higher education can also make for a richer, more satisfying intellectual and cultural life, but this facet of education was not mentioned by the doctor in our debate. But who says everyone must be a doctor, lawyer, or accountant in order to be happy? Why must we torture and stress children's talents and personalities in order to get them to fit into our rigidly square educational holes?

Because of our anxieties over our children's future, we have developed an intolerance for children's talents and temperamental diversity in America. Our fears over our children's future translate to high demands on our children today. And when they fail or underperform, it bothers us. It also very much bothers the children themselves. We justify our diagnoses of disorders and decisions to medicate by saying, "Our kids need these drugs to protect their self-image and self-esteem." Ironically, in the end we determine our normal children to be abnormal in order for them to be happy. These are the values and dynamics that drive the medication craze in America and that have me medicating Ned and children like him every day.

Money is the other factor that has me medicating Ned. Of course, I personally profit, but that's not what I mean. I could also make money by working with Ned's family or school, and I do. But I, along with every other doctor I know, am influenced these days by insurance companies. Insurance companies structure doctors' reimbursement so as to reward short visits, ones in which a prescription brings the session to a definitive conclusion. They discourage longer visits, and American doctors make much less money when they take the time to try to organize a coherent plan of action for a child. Such a plan—which might include medications but which also addresses parenting and educational needs—requires more time. Money also affects professional and public perceptions of drugs. Here, the all-powerful pharmaceutical industry dominates.

The drug industry hijacked American psychiatry in the 1990s.[12] In the process it came to determine the way American society thinks about children's problems. Since the mid-1980s, drug companies have dominated funding for all medical research. This is especially true in psychiatry: the companies have financial ties with virtually every psychiatric researcher and expert in their respective fields. They also influence doctors' education by paying for most physicians' continuing education after they graduate from medical school.

But the most radical shift occurred in 1997, when drug companies gained permission to advertise directly to patients in the mass media. In women's magazines and on television, advertisements ask if the viewer's child has difficulty completing homework. The root cause and solution, the advertisements suggest, are equally simple: a case of ADHD and treatment with a pill. This message reduces a complex socio-developmental undertaking like homework to a problem with the child's brain. Yet this message has been well received by the public, for several reasons. First, the "fix" is quick, relatively inexpensive, and safe. No one—not the student, teacher, or parent—is to blame for the problem. No one needs to make changes in lifestyles, expectations, or strategies. It's just the student's brain. To question otherwise is to risk the politically incorrect charge of holding parents, schools, or even children responsible.

The siren song of biological psychiatry fails to mention the lack of evidence for long-term effectiveness and safety for any of the psychiatric drugs given to children.[13] The stimulant drug I eventually prescribed for Ned has a seventy-year track record of short-term effectiveness and safety. However, in seventy years of use, there are still no studies showing that stimulants produce benefits that last through the end of adolescence or early adulthood. This doesn't mean the drugs aren't effective—they may be—but there is no proof.[14]

But beyond consideration of a drug's short-term effectiveness and safety, the fact that a drug "works" does not make it a moral equivalent of helping Ned's parents and teacher deal with Ned more effectively. Nor does medicating their child, even if safe, help them learn to respect Ned's particular balance of strengths and weaknesses—help them to appreciate Ned for who he is and not sand down the edges of his personality, forcing him to fit into a square hole.

From my training days onward, I've never been against the use of psychiatric medication for children. Despite my ethical qualms, I regularly prescribe stimulant drugs such as Ritalin to children. They do help children through difficult times. With much less frequency, I'll prescribe a drug like Prozac and, on rare occasions, even medicines like Risperdal. I've always been aware, however, of a potential ethical dilemma in their use. This problem isn't limited to child psychiatry or even to psychiatric drugs in general. Rather, the problem encompasses all therapeutics and goes to the core of medicine's role in society. This dilemma is more acute, though, in the case of children, who do not make the choice for themselves to take or not take a psychiatric drug.

With all the changes of the past twenty-five years—the about-face in psychiatric thinking, from blaming mothers to blaming the brain; the ever-increasing academic demands on children; and the drug industry's usurpation of American medicine—in one important way American medicine hasn't changed. With rare exceptions American medicine remains oblivious to public health and continues to focus on the pathology of the individual patient.[15]

All medical conditions stem from both biological (genetic and biochemical) and psychosocial (originating in emotions, culture, and society) factors. The importance of the relative roles of nature and nurture continue to be debated, but no serious scientist (except those promoting their own agenda) questions the contributions of both. Sophisticated and knowledgeable observers recognize that the influence of nature and nurture on each other is bidirectional, a two-way street. Most of us are aware of new brain-imaging studies that show changes in anatomy or function presumably responsibly for specific psychiatric disorders. We read in the newspaper of new studies, for example, demonstrating that the prefrontal cortex in children with ADHD is smaller than in those without the disorder. Less well-known are stunning brain-imaging examples that show how certain psychotherapies change brain metabolism and even anatomy as psychiatric disorders clinically improve with treatment.[16]

It's easier to appreciate the importance of environment on emotional and psychiatric problems, but even seemingly clear-cut medical conditions are influenced by the culture and society. A broken bone, for example, at first seems to be exclusively biological. The clinical picture is clear and confirmed by an x-ray. But if one examines the circumstances of accidents leading to broken bones (especially substance abuse and poverty), it is clear that emotional, social, and economic forces contribute to whose bones are more likely to get broken or fixed in the first place. And if broken bones have a place in public health, psychiatric issues should occupy a spotlight as well.

Some radical theorists have argued that psychiatric drugs are used to treat normal people who live in insane environments.[17] This position strikes me as both too facile and too broad to include all psychiatric problems. But a dysfunctional environment has particular relevancy when considering children's psychiatric problems. Children are much more dependent than adults upon their families, schools, and neighborhoods for, not the least, their ultimate physical survival. Ned's problem "exists" not only because of Ned's mix of personality and talents but also because that mix fails to meet the demands of his environment. Nor does his present environment precisely meet his needs. Thus, when I decide to medicate Ned, I know on some level that although I'm "helping" him, I've relieved any pressure on the system to adjust to him or otherwise address the uncomfortable questions posed by his intelligent but underperforming personality.

I know that for some cases of problem behavior in children, it's not likely that any environment could fully meet the needs of that child. Using medication as a practical intervention is warranted. But even in those cases, adding medication still decreases the burden on the system to meet the needs of the child. A school psychologist announced triumphantly at a meeting I attended that a third-grade girl I had just medicated was performing so much better that she no longer needed or qualified for extra help at the school. Although I am pleased about the girl's success, and I recognize that I have saved the school both time and money, I also wonder if I have done the right thing for the child long-term.

This ethical tension between helping the individual child and allowing for or permitting a socially irresponsible act becomes much stronger when I am obliged to treat much more normal-acting children like Ned and other dreamy, active, spunky, or rowdy kids with medications to help them "fit into" their respective families and schools.

When I try to explain why I continue to medicate the Neds of America with psychiatric drugs, I offer the following medical analogy. If as a pediatrician I were presented with an epidemic of serious diarrhea occurring in my community, of course I would treat these children with hydration, oral or intravenous fluids if necessary, and add other medications to help them get through their course of illness. But if I suspected that the epidemic was caused by drinking water that had been polluted by the effluent of an upstream factory, it would be unconscionable for me to remain silent. So I continue to medicate the Neds—and the Pippi Longstockings and Tom Sawyers too—of my community even as I try to raise consciousness and criticize aspects of our society and culture that contribute to the epidemic of psychiatric diagnosis and treatment in children.

We have chosen to make virtually any form of children's struggles or coping into one diagnosis or another. The absent-minded or active child becomes a child with ADHD. The shy or fearful child becomes one with generalized anxiety, social anxiety, or obsessive-compulsive disorder. Children who test their limits have oppositional defiant disorder, and those who really act up are quickly suspected of having bipolar disorder, the current "rage" diagnosis (pun intended) in our culture.

It is disquieting to see how rapidly parents, teachers, therapists, and doctors are ready to consider these diagnoses (virtually all of which presume some chemical imbalance to be addressed by a psychiatric medication) when children's behavioral problems continue for a little more than two or three weeks. But diagnosis of all these conditions is actively promoted by the medical-pharmaceutical industry. Discussions of the conditions are in the culture everywhere, from the PTA meetings to the plethora of parents' advice books (*The Explosive Child*,[18] *The Bipolar Child*,[19] and *The Out-of-Sync Child*[20] all focus on presumed brain pathology) to the daily diet of TV and print advertising touting a specific drug for a specific child disorder, and significant discussion also arises of course from the source of much useful and suspect information: the Internet.

The message is seductive and appealing, which explains in part its great cultural success. These diagnoses suggest that we know what's wrong with your child, and we have the specific treatment to cure it. Parents want the problem for their kids fixed as quickly, painlessly, and cheaply as possible. But mostly they want to protect their children's feelings, self-image, and self-esteem, so much talked about by experts as the psychological bottom line.

It seems not to matter that most of the medical and biological *DSM* world of diagnosis and treatment is smoke and mirrors. The diagnoses turn out not to be specific. Most children do not fit neatly into one category and rather display elements of a number of diagnoses. Maybe I should label Ned with NSD, "Ned Specific Disorder"? It would be more accurate. But furthermore, we still know very little about how the brain works in children (and adults), and categorizing children's behaviors contributes very little to our understanding of why kids are having problems. Finally, most of the medical treatments are nonspecific. Stimulants improve everyone's focus and attention.[21] The SSRIs (Prozac, for example) foster some resiliency for everyone (though not nearly as much for children as for adults). The anticonvulsants and antipsychotics "work" in bipolar disorder mostly by suppressing brain activity and all emotions (not just rage).

That is not to say that biology doesn't make contributions to behavior or that these drugs are without any benefit. Genetics and inherent biochemistry certainly make their influence known right from the start with infant temperament and childhood personality. Ask any grandmother, and she will tell you each child is different at birth. But genetics is not destiny, and biochemistry of the brain is quite reactive to the child's environment.

There is much discussion about the pedigrees of certain psychiatric conditions such as ADHD.[22] Now ADHD is said to run in families. Twin studies purport to separate genetic from environmental effects on the genesis of ADHD in any child. Supposedly, ADHD is as heritable as how tall you wind up to be (mostly based upon your parents' size).[23] But even these studies do not address the likely expression of a genetic condition. For example, phenylketonuria (or PKU) is a completely heritable metabolic neurological disease whose symptoms can be completely held at bay if the affected child eats a special diet.

Who's to say that children with a high-load genetic tendency toward ADHD, if treated with a "special" environment—say extra firmness and immediacy of consequences at a very early age (from perhaps twelve to thirty-six months)—would be able to *not* go on to express the full-blown syndrome. One more theory then, to explain the explosion of ADHD in America, considers society's relaxation of discipline in combination with an ongoing "genetic load" of ADHD in the population now showing itself as a fully expressed ADHD epidemic.

The psychiatric medications for children do have a place in treatment but are often chosen first or very early in treatment. They become a substitute for more effective work with parents and teachers. Direct therapy with children (as in play and even cognitive behavioral therapy) is overused and overrated as an effective treatment for most of the problems concerning parents. Too often a child has a prolonged course of ineffective individual psychotherapy only to be brought in to the doctor for what now seems to the parents, teacher, and therapist to be a brain problem, resistant to environmental influence. Not treating the child with medication at that point is likened to not treating a case of juvenile diabetes, akin to a form of medical neglect. Parents are highly sensitive to this self-criticism of "not having tried everything" to help their children. Given the dominant cultural position of childhood pathology as an explanation, it should be no surprise we choose disorder and medication to help our children as much as we do.

Some of my critics argue that I unnecessarily worry parents and children with my concerns about diagnosis and medication.[24] The rise in the rates of psychiatric diagnosis, they explain, is simply better medical practice. Doctors and the public are better informed about psychiatric conditions than they once were, and the stigma of psychiatric diagnosis has decreased. Earlier and broader diagnosis will prevent future worse problems. The drug industry is correctly educating doctors to recognize the signs of early but serious mental illness. Television ads "inform" the public and reduce the stigma of seeking help.

These medical experts with their drug-company affiliations (most medical research is now funded by the drug companies, and nearly all experts receive additional payments from drug companies to "educate" other doctors and the public[25]) make no mention of the broader social trends involved with childhood psychiatric disorders. But then again, the role of doctors is not to change the world, but to relieve pain and suffering, or so the argument goes.

I'm not sure I have sufficient answers for these leaders and spokespersons of today's child psychiatry. To be sure, there is a small group of children who would benefit from psychiatric medication even in the most ideal environments. I'd estimate those children to be less than 10 percent of those taking psychiatric drugs in America today.

And there's no proof behind the claim that early identification of mental illness will prevent it from worsening. But proponents of diagnosis and medication say we can't wait for such evidence—that many children are helped in the short term. My response comes from the Hippocratic Oath of doctors: "First do no harm." I acknowledge that seventy years of stimulant use offers us major reassurance that drugs like Ritalin represent only a small danger to children. But I'm not as sanguine or certain about any of the other drugs, such as Prozac, Depakote, or Risperdal—which we prescribe to millions of children with scant evidence of even short-term benefit and no guarantees of safety.

Also, the focus on treatment of children's mental health problems with medication—even when it helps in the short term—does not address the environmental factors that contribute to the problems. If anything, the use of medication makes it easier to ignore those problems. America, I'm afraid, will never commit the resources needed to meet the mental health needs of its children—even for the middle class. On that point, proponents of using medication in children have a valid but morally bankrupt argument.

Even if we were to shift our priorities toward assisting parents and schools in the raising of our kids, our unrealistic expectations would still have all children on the same track to the four-year college. Our "state religion" of corporate consumer fundamentalism—which holds that emotional happiness and satisfaction are based upon your income and how much you can buy or acquire—presents the four-year college degree as the best "guarantee."

Yet in our worry over their self-images, we forget that some of our children's best talents develop when they compensate for their weaknesses. We hear over and over again of so many personal testimonies from our greatest scholars, inventors, artists, and business leaders— how they struggled in school or in dealing with people early on, yet catapulted, often in their late teens and twenties, into fabulous productivity and self-satisfaction. We forget to appreciate our children's diversity of talent and temperament and instead worry about their differences and how they feel about themselves. We can try to medicate away their differences, but when we do, we are also removing what makes them human. Few parents would admit they want "perfect" children, but indeed, seeking that perfection comes in the name of protecting their children's self-esteem and decreasing their suffering. In this striving to protect and perfect, not only do we lose an appreciation of our children's uniqueness, but we also lose something of our own human experience as parents raising children we have successfully "perfected."

Of course it's difficult for parents to withdraw unilaterally from the race for academic achievement. We are all simply too afraid that our children will be left behind. Nor am I entirely suggesting we do withdraw altogether. But I do not see the possibility for any great shift in our mania for medicating away our children's problems unless some fundamental shifts occur in our broader values and attitudes in America. Ironically, it seems that only national adversity and tragedies, such as the Great Depression, World War II, or the destruction of the World Trade Center, temporarily slow our obsession with personal performance and ourselves.

Yet even within our current system of health care, we could decrease our reliance on psychiatric medication for kids by implementing some relatively painless changes. Involving fathers more in evaluations and treatment will simultaneously improve the effects of nondrug interventions and decrease the needs for medication. Any behavioral plan works better with both parents involved, and fathers continue to play a unique role in our culture both as role models and as more effective disciplinarians (political correctness aside, some stereotypes have validity). Ironically, even the course of medication for children will go better if and when fathers are involved and actively support that decision.

Ideologically and economically, doctors, especially children's mental health experts like child psychiatrists and behavioral/developmental pediatricians, have to be knocked off their office chairs. They need to go to their patients' schools and coordinate interventions between the teachers and parents. An organized, consistent educational and behavioral approach to children's problems involving the parents, the school, and the doctor offers the best chance that a program not requiring medications will succeed. The enormous prestige and power accorded these medical experts to effect change are wasted when the doctors remain in their offices simply diagnosing and medicating children.[26]

Still, the larger societal issues loom. Today, Ned will get his Ritalin drug. In two weeks he'll return happier. His teacher and parents will be pleased as well. Another Ritalin success story. I will smile and manage his drug use as effectively and safely as I can. But part of me feels wistful, sad, and even angry. Perhaps Ritalin will help him perform better in school, and Ned's childhood may be less painful on his way to adulthood. He may not feel especially stigmatized by the ADHD label and the need to take medicine (with so many kids taking medication, the stigma *has* decreased). My sadness comes because though Ned is a "good kid," he's not good enough to avoid the labels of mental pathology and the medications employed to treat them.

I have no doubt that Ned will be successful as an adult, because even as an eight-year-old he has a good heart. He's sensitive to others and knows how to be a good friend, even if he forgets to do his homework or can't find his keys, just like the absent-minded professor. I'm confident, in fact, that my labeling Ned with a disorder or medicating him will do little in the end to change that quality of his personality. But as I enter the second half of my medical career, I wonder if I will, at some point, see the last normal child—one who has not yet been characterized with one disorder or another and who is appreciated for who he or she is. And when I see him or her, will I medicate that child too?

2

Coca-Cola, McDonald's, and Ritalin*

According to legend, it was Cassandra's fate that her warnings over Greeks' bearing gifts went unheeded. The city of Troy failed to listen to its chief prophetess. They welcomed in the horse that was secretly filled with the Greek soldiers who later slaughtered the valiant defenders of Troy from within the walls of the city. These days, as a physician in the United States, I often feel like a Cassandra regarding the issues of attention-deficit/hyperactivity disorder (ADHD) and Ritalin use in America. I have practiced behavioral pediatrics in an affluent suburban community of the San Francisco Bay Area for twenty-plus years, evaluating and treating over 2,500 children for problems of behavior and learning at home and at school. I've prescribed Ritalin and other stimulants as part of a comprehensive treatment plan for many of these children.

Over the past fifteen years or so, the children presenting for an ADHD evaluation have become younger (and older) than the previous generation of elementary school children that I used to see and treat. Some are only three years old. Many more are girls. But most importantly, these children seem far less affected and less disabled than my earlier patients. I call them today's Tom Sawyers and Pippi

---

*A version of this chapter first appeared in French in *Enfances & Psy,* 2001.

Longstockings who are not meeting the expectations for children in modern-day America. Many of them are now taking Ritalin.

The trends I've experienced in my practice are mirrored in thousands of doctors' offices across the United States. Estimations vary widely on how many U.S. children take Ritalin, the best known of the stimulant drugs, or the others such as Dexedrine, Adderall, and now Concerta. I estimate that in 2005 about four and a half million children under eighteen took stimulants.[1] Possibly another four million or so adults also were prescribed Ritalin or its equivalent.[2]

Ritalin production rates are more accurate and have grown by 1,700 percent in the last fifteen years in the United States.[3] The change in generic amphetamine production during this period was an astounding 3,000 percent,[4] primarily as a result of a very aggressive and successful advertising campaign directed at physicians and consumers by Shire, a UK-based company that manufactures Adderall. America uses 80 percent of the world's stimulants.[5] What has been going on in the States? Are there any lessons for other countries and cultures just beginning their ADHD experience?

In the 1970s American psychiatry strongly embraced a biological/genetic/medical model as the explanation for maladaptive behavior. The introduction of Prozac in the late 1980s revolutionized the American public's acceptance of taking psychiatric drugs for relatively minor conditions ("cosmetic psychopharmacology"). A "chemical imbalance" to be treated by a drug became common terminology in the popular culture. In fact, in the early 1970s, a more insidious "living imbalance" began developing for American children.

The demands on children increased while their social supports from their families and school decreased. Children are now expected to learn more and at an earlier age. Both parents working became the norm for American families. Without extended family available, more and more young children must be in daylong day care settings, and older children become "latchkey" kids who are unsupervised in the afternoons until their parents get home.

Educational pressures on children and families became increasingly intense even as classroom size grew and funding for general education stagnated until very recently. A four-year college education or more is the ultimate goal for all American children these days to prepare them for competition in the global economy. In the process an intolerance for temperamental and talent diversity developed—all children, square- or round-pegged, must fit into the same rigid educational hole.

Attempts to control medical costs through the "managed care" movement in America only exacerbated the economic pressures on doctors to quickly address the problems of children with a "quick fix" drug. Parental authority has continued to erode in the United States as a form of politically correct parenting ironically has made punishment of children a "no-no" for fear of damaging children's self-image. All through the 1970s and 1980s, these socially combustible materials were gathering for a match to ignite the ADHD/Ritalin explosion.

The spark came in 1991 when federal administrators, under pressure from parent self-help groups and professional organizations, changed the criteria governing educational disability rights and services in America to include the ADHD diagnosis as a covered disability. Suddenly, parents looking to help their children in school sought medical evaluations for their children for ADHD in droves. In the process, many children received Ritalin for the first time, and the epidemic of ADHD in the United States began.

There are other societal factors that make the United States the most fertile "culture" medium for the growth of the ADHD/Ritalin virus, but one reason often mentioned doesn't hold up. A recent study found that children who watched more television between the ages of one and three were more likely to show evidence of ADHD at ages six and seven.[6] Thus, a "presto tempo" theory proposes that the rapid pace of life—with TV, faxes, pagers, and video games—leads to ADHD. However, American culture, at least in the cities, is not that much more "sped up" than, say, the urban cultures of Tokyo, Milan, or London. Yet in those cities rates of Ritalin use are one-tenth those of New York or Los Angeles.[7]

No other country offers economic-class mobility and opportunity like the United States. Here, everyone can be another Bill Gates, or so we are promised. We seem, as a culture, to be the least accepting of pain and sadness as part of normal life. Mourning and loss quickly become categorized as depression and need to be treated with medication. We have in our Declaration of Independence the right "to the pursuit of happiness," which in the late twentieth century became a mandate to be happy. If you are not happy, you must be depressed and need to be treated with a medication. Variations in childhood temperament and talent are treated as potentially early diseases—pre-morbid psychiatric or learning disorders—and in the middle and upper-middle class, they call for evaluation and treatment. In France and other European countries, a child's behavior may be more tolerated as "eccentric" and appreciated rather than seen as "deviant" and treated.

The pharmaceutical industry's influence on Ritalin sales cannot be specifically determined, but has likely been very significant in expanding the markets for Ritalin for both children and adults.[8] The drug companies didn't start the ADHD epidemic. Rather, the drug companies hijacked American psychiatry's ideological revolution of biology and medicine and promoted these views to physicians—and in the last eight years directly to consumers with magazine and television advertising. America is only one of two Western countries that allow direct-to-consumer advertising of pharmaceuticals.

Advertising for controlled abusable drugs is technically prohibited by an international drug treaty to which the United States is a signatory.[9] But in America, the freedom of speech argument for drug companies advertising Adderall or Concerta appears to have trumped international agreements. The U.S. government (specifically the Food and Drug Administration and the Drug Enforcement Administration) has sat quietly on the sidelines while the commercials continue to run.

Finally, there are consistent and inconsistent cultures. A consistent culture demands group conformity and cohesion at the expense of individual expression and gain. The best examples of consistent cultures are the Asian societies, including some of the Westernized countries such as Japan, Taiwan, and Hong Kong. An inconsistent culture prizes individual expression, self-promotion, and spontaneity while expecting conformity at school and work. The best example of an inconsistent culture is the United States. French attitudes may lie somewhere between the two extremes.

In America's inconsistent culture, we deliver a mixed message of promotion of self-expression but expectation to perform to our parents' and teachers' standards. The adults then act inconsistently and ambivalently when they make demands on the children. The result for a temperamentally vulnerable group of children, especially boys, is a weakened form of discipline that is insufficiently immediate or intense to help these children learn to self-regulate. They become symptomatic, are labeled as ADHD, and are treated with Ritalin.

As a physician, my job is to "ease suffering." After attempting to address issues of parenting and learning, I will prescribe Ritalin to children if their struggles continue. Ritalin allows anybody, child or adult, ADHD or not, to stick with tasks they find boring or difficult—the effects are not specific to those with ADHD. Ritalin use in children is relatively safe and well tolerated, though the long-term efficacy of Ritalin treatment alone for the problems of ADHD in childhood has never been proven. Neither is Ritalin, even if it "works," the moral equivalent to better parenting and schools for children.

However, my role as a citizen urges me to speak out about the larger social conditions and factors that have led to the ADHD/Ritalin epidemic in the United States. To not speak out would make me as a physician silently complicit with values and forces that I feel are harmful to children and their families. The way out of my professional ethical dilemma is to continue to prescribe medication but also to continue to alert others about this situation.

I have few illusions that my public questioning of Ritalin in the United States will do much to change our use of the drug. Our infatuation with performance enhancers such as Prozac, Ritalin, Viagra, and the anabolic steroids used illegally by professional athletes strikes right at the core of American values, which show little sign of changing at this time—for in America, more than anywhere else, we hold the belief that material acquisition will lead to emotional and spiritual contentment. We are, in the end, using Ritalin to prepare our tiny soldiers to enter the battle for the pursuit of money and the alleged happiness it brings.

Multinational pharmaceutical companies have targeted Australia and Western Europe as the next place to expand the stimulant market. American ADHD experts, nearly all receiving funds from the drug companies, proclaim the benefits of the ADHD diagnosis and treatment with Ritalin. Their data, framed in the simplistic, reductionistic medical model, appears impressive but never looks beyond the counting of children's symptom or pills. The living imbalance is never addressed.

With the collapse of Communism and the emergence of the heralded "New World Order," the American economic model and culture through economic globalism are certain to have power and influence across the world. The country and culture that has given the world Coca-Cola and McDonald's is now offering Ritalin. Many countries look at the United States with a mixture of envy and horror. Increased wealth certainly hasn't brought happiness to America.[10] Suicide rates and the incidence of mental illness continue to rise despite our economic success. Australia and Europe may well benefit from reexamining their positions on ADHD and medication in light of the American experience and take heed. Beware of Americans bearing gifts.

3

Gender, Power, and ADHD

Attention-deficit/hyperactivity disorder (ADHD or ADD for short) is the most common psychiatric disorder identified in children in the United States. Most studies estimate that 3 to 5 percent of American children meet official criteria for ADHD, though some respected experts suggest the rate is as high as 10 percent.[1] Over four million children take Ritalin (or its stimulant equivalents, Dexedrine or Adderall) for ADHD. Since 1991, production of stimulant medication for ADHD has soared by over 1,000 percent, and now toddlers, teens, and adults take Ritalin for a condition that was once pretty much a diagnosis of school-age boys.[2]

Literally thousands of scientific studies have examined virtually every nook and cranny of ADHD and its treatment.[3] Missing amid the welter of data on brain function, genetic pedigrees, and medication dosage is a satisfying explanation for a curious phenomenon of gender and age difference in the diagnosis of ADHD and the use of Ritalin. Of children who are referred to a doctor and subsequently diagnosed with ADHD, boys outnumber girls by about three or four to one (some have the ratio as high as nine to one).[4]

Informal surveys of adult ADHD clinics suggest a much more modest ratio of about 1.5 males to 1 female treated at these clinics. But more accurate data from a recent survey by Medco, a national private managed-care pharmacy company, goes beyond the word-of-mouth estimates from clinics specializing in ADHD treatment. Women actually represent a slight *majority* of patients being identified as

ADHD and treated with stimulants.[5] How can an ostensibly biological disorder affect boys more than girls, but women more than men? What happens to all those boys when they become adults? Does the condition disappear? And what about all these women with ADHD? Was their disorder simply missed in childhood, or could they develop it as adults?

Most of the research on gender differences in ADHD has involved children. The consensus is not surprising. Boys are referred to doctors more for ADHD than girls because they tend to be disruptive or oppositional.[6] They present class-management problems at school. Indeed, pressure from teachers and schools is the most common reason that families seek an ADHD evaluation for their children.

Girls tend to be identified later than boys. They also have problems in school, but the problems are more academic than behavioral. Girls are identified with the nonhyperactive, ADHD-inattentive type of problem more than boys are.[7] The girls show more anxiety and depression than the boys.

The underrepresentation of girls among the children being identified and treated for ADHD is generally perceived as a problem by many health research advocates for girls and women.[8] They feel there are gender differences between male and female ADHD that are not being recognized and appreciated.[9] They call for greater vigilance and publicity about girls with ADHD so as to increase identification of even minimally impaired girls.

Other ADHD experts respond that there are no real differences between ADHD boys and girls. Joseph Biederman, who heads Harvard's renowned Clinical and Research Program in Pediatric Psychopharmacology, has generated data on the nonreferred siblings of ADHD children who were identified at his clinic.[10] He used this group ostensibly to ascertain the characteristics of possible ADHD children in a community sample. He found in this nonreferred group three times as many boys meeting ADHD criteria as girls, but there were no differences in any of the psychoeducational or psychiatric measures between boys and girls in this sample.

The situation with adults is quite different. Here, as mentioned, the ratio between women and men is equal, with women slightly outnumbering men in treatment. Unlike the children who are brought in by their parents because the school is complaining, most adult ADHD candidates are self-referred. They come into clinics on their own seeking treatment.

Many of these women with ADHD are being diagnosed for the first time as adults. Critics of gender-neutral evaluations for ADHD, such as psychiatrist Patricia Quinn or psychologist Kathleen Nadeau, both practicing in the Washington, DC, area, believe that these women have had ADHD their whole lives and were missed or misdiagnosed because of their gender or sex roles.

Quinn offers a prototypic adult ADHD case in one of her articles.[11] Her example unintentionally reveals a point of view that perceives all underperformance as the result of a deficit or brain disorder. Her "Sarah" is a 23-year-old first-year law student. Sarah apparently always managed to do adequately or well in school, but it took her more time, or she needed the support of tutors or her mother. She managed a 3.0 GPA in college, but when she started law school, she felt overwhelmed. She simply didn't have enough time to study, eat, and sleep. Although her overall intelligence on testing was "superior," she had trouble with *language formulation, organization of information,* and *reading comprehension* (my italics—these are weaknesses in areas that could be rather critical for success in the study and practice of law).

Sarah was both stressed and depressed by her situation and thought she might have ADHD. Indeed, Dr. Quinn diagnosed her with the inattentive type of ADHD and began her on Concerta, a version of Ritalin whose effects last ten to twelve hours. However, Sarah's needs for studying went beyond twelve hours, so Dr. Quinn, in admittedly off-label use (not studied or officially approved by the FDA), allowed Sarah to take the medication twice a day. Sarah somehow managed to eat and sleep on this regimen, and her performance in law school did improve.

Later, apparently, Sarah also had Prozac added to her drug regimen to regulate mood fluctuations associated with her menstrual cycle. With these two drugs, Sarah was described as "stable" and "continued to do well without the need for additional psychotherapy."

But nowhere in this case description does Dr. Quinn wonder about or challenge whether Sarah's mixture of talents and temperaments is suited for a career in law. If Sarah were offered some counseling, she might come to consider her unhappy emotional state as a result of the clash between her desires and abilities rather than as ADHD or a brain disorder. Sarah may have chosen (after some appropriate grieving) to pursue another career that was satisfying but more compatible with who she was. Given her current direction, Sarah would seem to qualify for at least two psychiatric diagnoses and would need to take medication possibly for the rest of her life (or at least for as long as she practices law). We don't know whether these alternative options were ever discussed with Sarah. Rather, she is presented as a prototypical woman with heretofore-undiagnosed and untreated ADHD.

Most of the research about gender differences in the identification and treatment of ADHD in children and adults entirely avoids the larger societal roles males and females play at different stages in their lives with regard to issues of gender and power. Boys and girls (and also men and women) cope differently with stress. Stereotypically, whether by genetics or by culture or both, boys tend to "fight or flight" whereas girls "befriend or mend."

So boys, when stressed (primarily at school), try to take over the situation or punch someone. This does not sit well with authority figures (teachers, principals, police) who have the power to refer a boy to the school counselor or suggest a visit to the doctor for a "medical" evaluation. Girls, on the other hand, try to please or become invisible. In fact the learning problems of these girls go far more undiscovered compared with those of boys who are more disruptive and get the attention of the adults.

But an important shift occurs near the end of adolescence. After high school there are many more choices about what one can do to be productive and successful. There are more occupational niches that fit the squirmy boy who may find it difficult to stick with tasks that are boring at school but who focuses quite well on jobs he likes. "Hyper-focusing," that tendency to stick with things you like and ignore the demands of others, which has become a cardinal symptom of ADHD in schools, becomes a potential asset when the child, now teenager or adult, gets to choose what he wants to do.

ADHD boys frequently wind up working with their hands in the trades or working in the arts or entertainment business, in sales, or in start-up IPOs. Although demanding bosses still exist, there's usually another job available if the present one doesn't work out—more choice than for the struggling student stuck at school. Plus, the bosses are mostly other guys. Indeed, some ADHD boys become bosses and hire good administrators to keep them organized.

But for girls developing into women, things apparently become more difficult. Some of the learning problems that escaped scrutiny in the early grades have left them unprepared for high school (or a career in law). But more importantly, by gender or training, women have a harder time saying "no" or asking for what they want or need and continue to try to please. Women have added pressure in that they often now have responsibilities both inside and outside the home. Dad does help, but the bottom line is that mom is responsible for the kids, the food, and the house plus her job.

One mother, wife, and business exec I know, who was a bit disor-ganized but managed her mid-level career adequately, found the demands of her high-level promotion too much without the aid of

Ritalin. "It's hard to keep all those dishes spinning," she said breath-lessly, as I pictured her as one of those Chinese acrobats spinning plates at the end of long poles on the old Ed Sullivan show with Kachaturian's Saber Dances music playing in the background. The most difficult job I have in assessing adults for ADHD is deciding whether my patients—women in particular—are not completing their tasks because of distractibility, impulsivity, or disorganization or whether they simply have too many things to do. Ritalin helps in either case because its effects are not specific for those with ADHD; it can improve anyone's performance and it allows anyone, child or adult, ADHD or not, to stick with tasks they find boring or difficult.

Relative powerlessness and poverty among women lead to more self-referrals in general for mental health treatment, including for ADHD.[12] Ironically, the underrepresentation of girls in the child-hood ADHD population has led to a subspecialty within the field of ADHD—gender-based ADHD evaluations and treatment. But instead of more studies elucidating the hereditary and biology aspects of ADHD unique to girls or boys, I'm waiting for some research that analyzes the context and ecology of these potential problem personalities in the real world. I'm certain we'd learn a lot more about who has the power and control in the process.

4

Science, Ethics, and the Psychosocial Treatment of ADHD[*]

LAWRENCE DILLER AND SAM GOLDSTEIN

> No scientific undertakings or hypotheses are completely divorced from the social values of their time and place.
>
> *Russell A. Barkley, PhD*

Psychosocial treatments figure prominently in the guidelines for the treatment of ADHD from both the American Academy of Pediatrics[1] and the American Academy of Child and Adolescent Psychiatry.[2] But given the results of recent studies, are these recommendations simply political concessions to advocates of the "nurture" approach and to the biopsychosocial model? Will these psychosocial interventions appear as prominently in future versions of these guidelines? Are parents unfairly biased when they rate behavior therapy as more acceptable than medication for the treatment of their child's ADHD?[3] Is it

---

[*]A version of this chapter first appeared in the *Journal of Attention Disorders*, May 2006.

finally time to concede that psychosocial interventions add "nothing" to stimulant medication treatment and need not be pursued for uncomplicated ADHD, as some prominent recent reviews have suggested?[4] The answers to these and related questions, though important for individual families, also have great implications for social policy (e.g., funding of schools, parenting programs, or treatment modalities). It is assumed that the answers to these questions are known and in a fair and reasoned way guiding such policy. Indeed, for the most part the answers are neither known nor guiding policy.

More than one hundred studies demonstrate that parent- and teacher-training programs improve child compliance, reduce disruptive behaviors, and improve parent–child and teacher–child interactions.[5] Though a number of short-term studies have scientifically demonstrated the effectiveness of psychosocial interventions for ADHD,[6] the case for medication's exclusive status in ADHD treatment derives from two major studies. The first is the ongoing National Institute of Mental Health ADHD Treatment (MTA) study of 600 children.[7] Three years after the initial MTA results were published, Klein et al. published a series of articles reviewing their study of 103 children over a three-year period.[8] A multisite population of highly screened, well-diagnosed, impaired children with ADHD characterized the subjects of both studies. Most importantly, unlike previous long-term research on ADHD, children in both studies *were randomized* into medication-only, combined-treatment, and community-treatment groups.

The initial "headlines" from the MTA study emphasized that the group of those under combined medication and psychosocial treatment did no better than the medication-only group. However, further analysis of the data indicated that this was true only for the minority of children with uncomplicated ADHD.[9] The majority of participants diagnosed with ADHD also had comorbid ODD, anxiety, or both. Adding the psychosocial component for these youth to medication treatment statistically improved outcomes compared with the results for the medication-only group.[10] Data collected after two years tended to further diminish the superiority of the medicated groups (alone or in combination) over the psychosocial-only and community-based service groups for all the children in the study.[11]

The subsequent study completed in New York City and Montreal was firmer in its conclusions about the lack of increased benefits in adding psychosocial treatment to the effects of medication alone. Over a variety of parameters (e.g., academic achievement, socialization, emotional status, and parent practices) the conclusions were the same. The authors were quite clear about the lack of benefits from psychosocial interventions for ADHD when medication was employed.

These two studies appear to drive the final nail into psychosocial treatment's coffin. Despite current APA and AACAP guidelines suggesting equality between treatment choices, these studies are being used to promote a medication-first approach to ADHD. An MTA research paper was mailed to pediatricians and child psychiatrists in the United States by one of the manufacturers of a medication used to treat ADHD. But whether or not, on medical or moral grounds, medication should be the primary approach in a community-diagnosed population with ADHD remains unclear.

CATEGORY VERSUS DIMENSION

As a defined condition in the *DSM-IV-TR*, ADHD represents a category, but the symptoms of ADHD are clearly dimensional in nature. Who exactly are the children with ADHD making up the subject pool in published research, which ultimately guides clinical practice? Are they the more severely symptomatic and impaired? It is likely that a more rigid and stringent application of *DSM* criteria is applied to children participating in peer-reviewed and published research studies.[12] Children in these studies may also be more symptomatic and impaired than children in the community. Further, data on who receives medication in the community is inconsistent and confusing. Epidemiological studies suggest that overall these medications are not necessarily overprescribed,[13] but their use is increasing.[14] It seems that in "real world" practice, ADHD is often missed.[15] Stimulants are usually prescribed for the most impaired,[16] but as much as half the time, stimulants may be prescribed for children who don't meet full *DSM* criteria for the ADHD diagnosis.[17]

Further, in severe cases of ADHD, the effects of psychosocial interventions may not be as obvious. But the same may not be true for children with borderline or mild ADHD. This group of less impaired children, given the bell-shaped distribution and dimensional nature of the symptoms of ADHD, surely represent the majority of the cases a community-based clinician might treat. Various studies suggest that behavioral approaches do work with ADHD.[18] Studies have also demonstrated that with greater intensity of psychosocial interventions comes reduction in the amount of stimulant medication necessary to control symptoms.[19] Medication "works," but when given as the first treatment, it may obscure the benefits of psychosocial interventions. Even in the MTA and Klein studies, which found no statistically significant improvements when psychosocial treatments were added, the authors reported that parents from the groups with the combined-treatment approach developed not only a better understanding of their children, but also a better feeling for them.

The behavior of these children might not have been that different before and after behavioral training, but parents' attitudes could have fundamentally changed. Perhaps these parents developed a better sense of the problem and a perception of increased control over their children. *DSM*-based research would only focus on the symptoms of the child and equate symptom relief with improvement.[20] Impairment, an even more elusive quality, however, may indeed decrease even without any overall symptom change, in that impairment is a function of the children's behavior within the context of the environment's expectations and responses. Parental attitudes and behavior may well immediately affect measures of impairment, and measures of children's behavior may remain the same or improve slowly over time. Indeed, the notion of "problem" is more closely tied to impairment than to symptoms, a point often lost or obscured in mainstream *DSM*-based research.[21]

SCIENCE, ETHICS, AND ADHD

Science is about proof, replication, and utility. Yet the "scientific" discussion on ADHD has rarely focused on moral and ethical issues as we decide the best course of action for children with developmental disabilities. We do not disagree with the science that has demonstrated that stimulant medications are efficacious in assisting and addressing the needs of children with ADHD, their families, and their schools. We are, however, uneasy about the use of medication as the first and only treatment for the vast majority of cases of ADHD, particularly in the absence of convincing longitudinal data suggesting that symptom relief alone changes future lives for the better. Children's positive response to stimulant medication is not equivalent to an improvement in their environment and future by assisting their parents, schools, and general communities. Though medication treatment is cost-effective and may be all that is needed in the short term to reduce symptoms and impairment for many children with ADHD, we recognize the logical fallacy of making medication, even when effective, the equivalent of psychosocial interventions.

The universal enhancing effects of stimulant medications are critical for moderately and severely impaired children with ADHD. But substituting the ubiquitous effects of stimulants (out of cost, speed, or convenience) for psychosocial interventions in the case of borderline to mildly impaired children with ADHD is morally dubious. In addition there are side effects to these medications along with unanswered questions about long-term outcomes. Though some children will do fine with stimulant medication alone, shouldn't their parents at least be given better "operating instructions" for their children?

WHERE DO WE GO FROM HERE?

Despite seventy years of stimulant use in psychiatry, we still do not know for certain the best long-term treatments for ADHD. Pills are no substitute for skills; symptom relief is not the equivalent of changing long-term outcome for the better. Children with ADHD do in fact learn to self-regulate, albeit not as quickly as others. They need more practice. Practice facilitates proficiency. No one would argue this is not the case. It is much better for them if they can learn to self-regulate within the confines of their homes under the loving guidance and caring supervision of their parents rather than outside of the home in the communities we have created, communities that hold so many potential adversities for them.[22]

Though we are reassured by a number of brief meta-analytic studies of the efficacy and safety of long-term stimulant use,[23] we may never know for sure whether medication use is safe and effective through multiple decades of life. Do psychosocial interventions add anything to medication? This too we may never know for sure, when ADHD is equated with a broad base of life and family issues. Without a definitive answer, we are not prepared to abandon parenting and educational strategies for medication alone. We acknowledge that even the strongest advocates for medication use for children with ADHD would not argue for this approach. Yet when studies conclude that psychosocial interventions add little or nothing to the treatment of ADHD, we worry about the implications of such a message on public policy and its effects on the professional and lay communities.

Finally, human beings should not be defined by their handicapping conditions, but rather their conditions should be understood within the broader context of the forces that shape their lives. This leads us to question the means by which we apply evidence-based or scientifically validated treatments within the broader community. Because psychosocial treatments, particularly psychotherapy, are directed not just at providing symptom relief or changing behavior but at changing thinking as well, it is worth addressing the case for psychosocial treatments for conditions such as ADHD.

The debate over psychosocial treatments versus medication has profound implications for the way our society decides to view and treat children with emotional, behavior, and performance problems. The controversy over treatments for ADHD is yet another iteration of the nature–nurture debate. With ADHD, researchers and leaders in the field of child psychiatry, psychology, and pediatrics continue to fight a rearguard battle against the legacy of a half a century of the "mother blaming" associated with the Freudian hegemony in our society. Although remnants of the Freudian model remain viable, it is time to declare the battle over. However, insisting that the basis for behavior in children and adults is only biological and driven by heredity is simplistic and reductionistic and in fact does not fit the emerging research concerning gene–environment interaction.[24] Psychosocial treatments for ADHD have consequently suffered despite their promise,[25] perhaps in part in because we have failed as a field to develop a comprehensive program that includes the stock dividends or equity that come with the corporate entities that manufacture and promote medication. But at this point, it also seems like overkill—bad for children and bad for society—to imply in one way or another over and over again that "parenting doesn't matter." Advocating for psychosocial treatments for ADHD is not simply a matter of political correctness. It is the ethical recognition of a moral and clinical reality that for most children with ADHD, a combination of psychosocial and medical interventions will best serve their present and future needs.

5

When Does a Right
Become Wrong? Unflagging
Accommodated SAT Scores

Over my decades of practice in behavioral/developmental pediatrics, I've noticed certain seasonal trends in referrals for consultation and treatment. For example, telephone calls for new appointments tend to slow down in mid-June, at the end of the school year. I imagine Johnny's mother thinking, "Thank God summer is almost here. Maybe his behavior will improve." Not surprisingly, with the start of school in late August, my phone begins to ring more frequently.

However, in recent years I've noticed a mini-uptick in the number of calls I receive about a month or two before the Scholastic Aptitude Test (SAT) is administered, which usually happens in late October and March. Therefore, I wasn't too surprised when Howard Leary, father of Katie, a high school senior, left a frantic message on my answering machine. "Dr. Diller, you saw Katie six years ago, and we really need to get in to see you as soon as possible. We're thinking again that Katie should take Ritalin, and we'd like to have a prescription before she takes the SAT in three weeks." I appreciated Howard's candor and directness. Often parents (and children) are less direct in their bottom-line request, but I had met this child and her family years ago, so I wasn't too put off by Howard's style.

Though I remembered Howard as an intense, successful local attorney, I had only a vague sense of Katie. So before I returned Howard's call, I checked my case notes, which covered a few visits in 1999, and they helped sharpen my memories of Katie and her family. Katie was a gangly, somewhat awkward middle-schooler at that time, a little bit bigger and a little bit more uncertain than most children her age. At eleven, after repeated operations to repair a clubfoot, she could walk without a limp, but I wondered whether the extended treatment had affected her confidence. I noted that her parents were concerned about her school performance and whether she had the nonhyperactive form of ADHD. In my office, all her academic skills seemed to be at or above grade level, but her teacher had said that her performance was "hot/cold." Katie frequently seemed surprised when called upon in class, but her teacher couldn't decide whether she hadn't been paying attention or was anxious, or both.

My assessment was similar. I felt, however, that the anxiety component was the greater of the two factors, leading to Katie's inattentiveness and giggling when she was called upon in class. Whatever the cause, I thought Katie's problems were mild six years ago, and the teacher agreed. I offered the parents a behavior plan for Katie and the suggestion that if she didn't improve, Ritalin could be considered a few months down the line.

About two weeks after that visit, Howard called me again, asking for advice on how to use Ritalin for Katie. Almost immediately after my evaluation, they had gone to another "ADHD doctor," Dr. Riordan, known locally to other professionals for prescribing the drug to virtually all the children he saw. Dr. Riordan had decided that Katie had a mild case of ADHD and had prescribed the stimulant, but without explaining to the parents the subtleties of a titration trial or even mentioning many of the drug's adverse effects.

I must admit that I was a bit chagrined by Howard's request and asked him why he wasn't calling Riordan for the information. Howard said that they liked me better and that I had a better communication style. After a mental shrug, I told the parents to come in, and when they did, I went over the details of using Ritalin effectively and safely. I didn't hear from the Learys again until Howard's call six years later.

Upon meeting Katie again, who was now a high school senior, I was struck by how much more self-assured she seemed in comparison with her middle-school days. She said she took Ritalin for a while in sixth grade, but didn't care for it: "I felt like I was in a dream state. It made me feel crazy." Interestingly, Katie actually had very good grades all through middle school. However, at the beginning of her freshman year at the local (high-performing) high school, Katie's performance began to slip. She readily admitted that she had not been particularly motivated about schoolwork and had become much more interested in her friends and boys.

I met Katie alone one time and asked her why she was interested in taking Ritalin again. She said she wanted to go to college, but she and her parents thought her B grade point average (GPA) would keep her out of the best state universities and public four-year colleges. "Why do you want to go to college in the first place?" I asked. She was quite clear: "I want to get away from my parents and home. It isn't bad at home, but I want to have more freedom and be on my own."

I queried her a little more deeply on what she wanted to achieve by going away to school. Her answer surprised me: "I want a college with a good beach." Not unlike her father, Katie was direct. Her long-term ambitions were to travel, and she admitted that she had little interest in academics. When pressed about her current classes, she said, "I like photography." She didn't seem the least bit embarrassed about her desires or her nonacademic interests when it came to why she wanted to go to college.

Her renewed consideration of Ritalin had arisen because she was concerned that a particular southern California college with a very good beach would not accept her with her overall GPA unless she did well on her SAT. On her first go-around, she had struggled to finish the verbal and math sections in time. She admitted that she "fudged the times" when she took the practice SAT exams (part of the private-preparation tutoring programs that seem to be de rigueur these days for every middle- and upper-middle-class high school student). She hoped that the Ritalin would improve her performance even though years ago, she hadn't liked its effects.

The test was only three weeks away, which is why Katie and her parents were rushing now. They wanted to make sure, before she took it on exam day, that the medication had the desired result and no serious adverse effects. I felt very uneasy about the situation. I had not had the impression that her symptoms were serious when I had met and evaluated her six years earlier, and now, I thought even more strongly that her motivation—or lack of it, when it came to academics—was more of a factor than it had been when Katie was in middle school. I was worried about Katie's passivity and her desire to "take a pill" in order to help her quest for the college with the best beach. I also suspected that Katie's passivity was a screen masking some of her anger at the whole process which "forced" her to have to go to school in the first place and fit into these rigid academic and career roles.

When I voiced my concerns to Katie and her parents, they did not challenge my analysis; they even agreed with it. I could tell that her parents were actually more ambivalent about Katie's taking medication than Katie was herself. (This isn't an uncommon situation these days with the teens who come to my office to "get meds.") I even mentioned some private two-year community colleges in southern California with "good beaches" that virtually anyone could attend, despite mediocre grades or SAT scores. But Katie was adamant; she wanted to try medication.

The diagnosis of ADHD-inattentive type—the type of attentional disorder without a hyperactivity or impulsivity component—is a slippery slope. In my experience, such children (or adults) almost always have a learning or processing problem in addition to attentional issues. In fact, I, along with many others, believe that the attentional problems are secondary to the learning difficulties because most of the time, these kids do quite well in all areas outside of academics. This group of ADHD-diagnosed kids is becoming the majority of those diagnosed in adolescence, and they are the ones whose diagnoses arouse the greatest controversy (see "In the Valley of Motivational Fatigue," Chapter 10).

Since problems of motivation are at the core of the conceptualization of ADHD, if I had wanted to, I could have talked myself into believing Katie had a mild case of ADHD-inattentive type. But in reality, the immediate question was more practical: should I write a prescription to help Katie before the SAT?

Ultimately, I decided that I would. The tipping point was my experience with Katie six years earlier. I knew then that she was, at best, a borderline case, and she probably was now as well. If I had met her for the first time at seventeen, I would have been less likely to offer her a prescription. But considering my last go-around with the family, I knew that if I said "no," there was a high chance they would go back to Dr. Riordan for another prescription.

We decided that Katie should try Adderall XR in ascending dosages over the next couple of days. I suggested Adderall because it was amphetamine, and Katie's previous negative experience on stimulants was with Ritalin, which is methylphenidate. Five days later, I received another call from Howard. Once again, Katie didn't like the effects of the medication, so she stopped taking it. And it appeared that my discussions with the family had led Katie to question what she wanted to do and where she wanted to go. She was still likely to try college, but didn't think taking medication to get into a particular school was worth it.

It's possible that Katie wound up taking the SAT with extra time, the most common accommodation offered to students who have medically proven physical or learning disabilities, though I don't know if that was the case for Katie. Katie didn't ask me to evaluate her for the ADHD disability status required to be granted the extra time. Her sophisticated parents probably knew that I don't routinely do the hours of psychoeducational testing required to meet the disability criteria required by the Educational Testing Service (ETS), which administers the SAT as well as other academic qualifying exams.

Furthermore, coming to an evaluator three weeks before the exams would not have given ETS—which requires at least two months to evaluate a student's application for disability status—enough time to process the request. As Wayne Camara, ETS's vice president for research, told me in two extended telephone conversations,[1] the testing service would be highly skeptical and would scrutinize very carefully the "credentials" of any student who tried to claim ADHD just weeks before the exam.

Dr. Camara has spent many years at ETS, and his pride and belief in the SAT comes through in conversation. The SAT was initially developed after World War II as a way to "level the playing field" by allowing students from public high schools to demonstrate their abilities on the same basis as those from elite prep schools. In 2005 nearly 1.5 million high school students took the SAT, equal to the number of students entering their freshmen year at four-year colleges.[2] Because the SAT score and the student's high school GPA have been studied and adjusted extensively in an effort to predict a college freshman's GPA at the end of the first year, the SAT has become an invaluable tool for college admissions officers. And despite admission officers' attempts to downplay the importance of the scores for acceptance at their schools, parents and students know intuitively that this is not the case. Though it is likely that few students are denied college admission solely because of a low SAT score, even the University of California, Berkeley, which publicly de-emphasizes its reliance on the SAT, requires a minimum combined score of 1,100 out of 1,600[3] potential points to be considered for admission.[4]

In recent years, there's been controversy regarding the continued relevance of the SAT. Indeed, the test has been changed somewhat; among other things, a writing sample is now required. But one change that has gone relatively unnoticed will, in my opinion, cause confusion and resentment as more students learn about it.

Disabled students who took the SAT in October 2003 were the first to not have their scores "flagged" (marked with an asterisk, which indicated that the test had been taken under nonstandard conditions—almost always, extra time) when their scores were reported to admitting colleges. ETS had been offering accommodations to the disabled since the early 1980s, but their test scores were flagged. Then, in 2002, under legal pressure from two disability rights groups, ETS decided to discontinue the practice. The whys and wherefores of this decision illuminate the quandaries and ethics of academic performance, learning disabilities, and the law at the start of the twenty-first century in America.[5]

The movement for rights for the disabled comes from the same core American social and legal values that inspired the American civil rights movement in the 1950s and 1960s. The movement for rights for the disabled gathered strength in the 1980s and culminated with the passage of the Americans with Disabilities Act (ADA) in 1990. Educational reforms for the disabled were also embodied in legal reinterpretations of Section 504 of the Vocational Rehabilitation Act of 1973 and the Individuals with Disabilities Education Act (IDEA) of 1990, which has since been reauthorized by Congress every seven years.

All these laws are intended to level the proverbial playing field in areas of employment and education for the disabled. Some reports estimate that up to 10 percent of the population may qualify for disabled status based on one or another set of criteria.[6] When it comes to admission to a college, an individual must demonstrate that he or she is qualified despite the disability. "Reasonable" accommodations must be made under the law, both in the qualifying test-taking and in admissions, without compromising the school's and the test's basic standards. However, once these standards have been modified for the disabled, then further identification of that student—say, by flagging the nonstandard conditions of an accommodated SAT test—potentially allow colleges to discriminate against the civil rights of that student. Such practices are specifically prohibited by the ADA and Section 504.

Or so the argument goes. And that's what led the two disability rights organizations to sue ETS and the College Board in the late 1990s to abandon the "flag." Disability rights groups had already successfully forced a settlement over ETS's Graduate Math Aptitude Test (GMAT). But ETS was uneasy about lowering the standards of the SAT and thus decreasing its value to colleges in predicting freshman performance. Still, the writing appeared to be on the wall, so in 2002 both parties agreed to the formation of a seven-member panel of experts who would review the "evidence" and offer a solution to the rights groups' challenge.

An accommodation for a disability should legally allow the student to perform at his or her ability level without compromising the constructs of the test. Thus, it would appear to be less of a problem to allow a student with cerebral palsy (CP) who has difficulty handling a pencil to have someone fill in the circles on a multiple-choice test.

Making the test available in Braille for a blind person is another non-controversial accommodation. However, offering extra time (either 50 or 100 percent more) for learning disabled (LD) students—a group which includes ADHD students as a subcategory—was far more controversial on two counts.

First, the nature of learning disabilities is more interpretative and less tangible than CP or blindness. Paper/pencil psychometric tests can draw a statistical line on a continuum from normal to abnormal performance that supposedly differentiates abilities as a "disorder" for some LD diagnoses. There are, of course, fairly objective physical dimensions to CP and blindness. But for ADHD, there aren't even absolute psychometric standards. The official identification is made by an "expert" using a variety of psychometric tests and questionnaires, none of which alone offers a diagnostic gold standard. The questionnaires—which ask questions like, "Do you fidget not at all, a little bit, or a lot?"—are directed to the student, a parent, and the student's teacher and are almost completely subjective by nature. Although severe and even moderate ADHD might not be too difficult to diagnose, mild ADHD, especially the inattentive type, is wide open to interpretation as to what behavior crosses the line from a variation of normal to the deviancy of "disorder." And given that in the general population, the ability or lack of ability to "attend" or "concentrate" is distributed as a bell-shaped curve, the vast majority of diagnosed ADHD cases will necessarily be of the mild variety.

This interpretative aspect of LDs (particularly of ADHD) is borne out by epidemiology, both when assessed in the general community and when measured by those granted accommodations for the SAT. In both situations, affluent white male students predominate in the LD/ADHD population.[7] In reality, it is not the case that wealthy white males are actually more frequently disabled. Rather, their families are more likely to be interested and able to seek private evaluations for them in order to have them diagnosed with ADHD and granted disability status. The reasons for this disparity are complex and sociocultural rather than neurodevelopmental in nature.[8] But clearly, the possibility exists for abuse of the disability status accommodations by wealthier, more sophisticated families. Furthermore, a situation of de facto discrimination exists against the less affluent, particularly against minority students who aren't identified as disabled publicly by their school districts or privately by their families.

This is not just a theoretical issue. It takes on increasing urgency because of the greater and greater number of students seeking disability/extra-time status for the SAT. Between 1990 and 1999, the number of students taking the nonstandard versions of the SAT tripled.[9] The percentage of disabled students qualifying under LD (which includes ADHD) went from 15 percent to 41 percent in that time.[10] No other category of disability had increases during this same period. Now, with the possibility that the disability status of students who took the nonstandard versions of the SAT due to their disability would not even be revealed to the colleges those students applied to, ETS was deeply concerned that the floodgates would open even wider—that even more students would to try to obtain LD/disability status in order to be accommodated during the SAT and thus perform better on it.

The second area of concern for ETS was whether allowing increased time for the disabled truly changed the nature of what the SAT was testing. The disability rights groups argued that in a timed test, the need for speed interfered with the disabled students' opportunity to demonstrate their ability. (On purely theoretical grounds, someone with ADHD, who generally has trouble with delayed consequences, might actually do better with smaller, more immediate deadlines within the test, rather than simply with an increased allotment of time.) However, ETS research showed that "disabled" students who were given more time generally increased their combined SAT (math and verbal) scores by about seventy points.[11] On average, "abled" or normal students given the same amount of increased time improved their scores by only twelve points, which is not statistically significant. Even with the additional time, disabled students tended to perform about sixty points lower on average in the combined scores than those students considered "normal." These performance differences, or lack of them, proved critical to the panel of experts.

The blue-ribbon panel convened over a period of two days in New York in 2002, presided over by an attorney. In a nonbinding recommendation, they voted four to two (the chair of the panel was a nonvoting member) to remove the flagging of nonstandard test-takers' scores.[12] At the time, the decision generated minimal media coverage. However, all high school advisors and college admissions officers were quite aware of the change. Neither they nor ETS knew for sure what kind of impact the change would have on the disabled or on the admissions process.

In fact, the anticipated flood of students qualifying for disability status has not occurred; the number of qualified disabled students has actually gone down somewhat, from about 32,000 in 2003 to 30,000 in 2005.[13] Dr. Camara explained that even as ETS removed the flag, it decided to strengthen and tighten the criteria for approving the disability status of test takers. ETS has also increased its vigilance regarding abuses of the diagnosis. Dr. Camara cited an instance wherein an elite Eastern prep school was warned that their 20 percent rate of students diagnosed as disabled was far beyond what could be expected (and approved) by ETS.

Notwithstanding the continuing possibilities of abuse of the diagnosis, there are aspects of the nonflagging decision that remain unsettling. One of them is the ETS research conclusion that increasing the time allotment for the ordinary student doesn't change anything. This conclusion flies in the face of the experience of nearly every student who has taken the SAT (including my two teenage sons and me), every professional SAT coach, and such test-preparation companies as Kaplan Test Prep and Princeton Review. ETS doesn't like to admit that a person can "cram" for the SAT because it's supposed to be a test of overall learning and innate ability. But even Dr. Camara admits that taking practice tests will improve a student's performance and test scores, and he recommends doing it.

Taking practice tests helps both by familiarizing the student with the kinds of questions asked and by making the student aware of time management, according to Eric Myers, a Bay Area professional preparer for the last eighteen years.[14] "Time does make a big difference," he says. "Pacing is very important, even if it means not finishing the test." Like many who help students prepare for these types of tests, Myers recommends taking a pass on difficult questions and returning to them if there is time. He suspects that the time limit doesn't matter very much to the upper-echelon students, but it does present a major hurdle for the average student.

This leads to an interesting conundrum. If a "normally abled" student first took the test in the standard amount of time and then was allowed extra time to take it again, and his scores improved by seventy or more points, would the improvement in his scores suggest that he had previously undiagnosed LD or ADHD? My sixteen-year-old just took the PSAT (Preliminary SAT) and didn't finish parts of the test. When his results came, he felt he did poorly compared with his friends. Could he have LD or ADHD right under my behavioral pediatrician's nose? Should I have him tested (at a cost of about $2,000 on average)? In his case, I suspect he just needs more practice taking the test, as Dr. Camara suggested.

But if indeed adding extra time for the standard student doesn't change his test scores, as ETS claims, why limit that student to the standard time if he or she requests extra time? Dr. Camara admits there would be no technical or ethical reason for refusing the request. It turns out that the standard time period continues to be used primarily for logistical and business reasons (i.e., cost), all of which sets up the current ETS protocol on extra time for a Bakke-like court challenge.

Allan Bakke, you may recall, was the celebrated (or infamous, depending upon your politics) young man who, when refused admission to medical school, sued the Regents of the University of California over their affirmative action program and the race-based component of their admissions policy, claiming that as a white male, he had been discriminated against when his application to medical school was denied.[15] Ultimately, the Supreme Court, applying the "equal protection clause" of the 14th amendment, ruled that schools couldn't use race to improve a previously unfair admissions policy. The situation concerning the abled and disabled is not entirely analogous to racial issues, but given the ambiguities of the LD diagnosis, de facto discrimination against less affluent families in access to diagnosis, and overt contradictions between ETS data on extra time for "normal" students and the experience of virtually anyone who has taken the test—that time matters—it is only a matter of time before someone challenges ETS in a legal forum when they are denied admission to the college of their choice on the basis of their SAT scores.

It will be interesting to see how the judicial system evaluates the data. If the legal record on disability rights in employment is any guide, the rights activists should be concerned. In disability suits, juries have repeatedly sided with employers, apparently reflecting their sense either that the employee was not qualified for the job in the first place or that the weaknesses the employee manifested were not the result of a legitimate disability.

Don't get me wrong. I feel great progress has been made in our society in giving a certain population with different temperaments and talents the opportunity to contribute to society at their optimal ability. Everyone gains in that situation. I'm in strong support of each individual pursuing his or her talents to the fullest possible extent. But the controversy over deflagging the SAT scores of students accommodated due to their disability statuses involves other disturbing issues of achievement and success in America, potentially trivializing the disorders, efforts, and rights of the truly disabled.

Katie was just one of many high school students who do not know what they want to do after high school but who feel they must go to college. I know other students who *do* know what they want—to become a doctor, engineer, or lawyer, perhaps—but whose talents clearly are not suited for those careers. Although we hear mostly about the success stories—of LD or ADHD students who "made it" to law or medical school and of lawyers who are dyslexic and practicing—the actual statistics on LD students in higher education are sobering.

Graduation rates from four-year colleges are quite low for LD students, and most LD students go to junior colleges.[16] Rates of psychiatric drug use in colleges are skyrocketing. Estimates are that 25 to 50 percent of college students reporting to university health services take a psychiatric medication, usually a Ritalin- or Prozac-type drug.[17] I believe a large proportion of this legal drug use arises because of the pressures and stresses faced by kids who either don't belong in or really don't want traditional higher education. By accommodating and deflagging, are we doing these students any favors? Or should someone be directing these young people to fields in which they can earn decent incomes and make valuable contributions to society without trying to squeeze their round or octagonal personalities and talents into increasingly rigid square holes?

Nearly everyone should have some post-high school training or education. Several of my most "successful" ADHD patients received automotive or aircraft repair training and immediately found well-paying jobs in the area. Another found his niche, not only vocationally but socially, and then landed a job at Pixar Animation Studios. However, these trajectories do not initially offer the social cachet and economic security ostensibly connected to a four-year bachelor's degree.

I hope I hear from Katie or her parents again, ideally in about ten years. That would be enough time to know with far more certainty how she fared in school and to get a better sense of her long-term life path. I suspect she will wind up much like her parents; her mother finished college, but, supported by her attorney husband, she devoted most of her adult life to raising children, an honorable endeavor. Given the general demands of today's economic environment, which requires two incomes to stay even, Katie may have to do more juggling. But I seriously doubt she will pursue a career that calls for a long-term commitment to academics. It really isn't a major part of her talent or temperament. However, at seventeen, she doesn't know that, and she feels she has no choice. She thinks she must fit into that square hole.

Part II

One Pill Makes You Larger: Stories from the Real World of Families Coping with Children's Behavior and Psychiatric Drugs

6

Just Say Yes to Ritalin!*

Public school administrators, long the enthusiastic adherents to a "just say no" policy on drug use, have a new motto for the parents of certain tiny soldiers in the war on drugs: Medicate or Else! It is a new and troubling twist in the psychiatric drugs saga, in which public schools have begun to issue ultimatums to parents of hard-to-handle kids, saying they will not allow students to attend conventional classes unless they are medicated. In the most extreme cases, parents unwilling to give their kids drugs are being reported by their schools to local offices of child protective services, the implication being that by withholding drugs, the parents are guilty of neglect.

At least two families with children in schools near Albany, New York, recently were reported by school officials to local CPS offices when the parents decided, independently, to stop giving their children medication for attention-deficit/hyperactivity disorder.[1] (The parents of one student pulled him from school; the other set of parents decided to put their boy back on medication so that he could continue at his school.)

As a doctor with a practice in behavioral pediatrics—and as one who prescribes Ritalin for children—I am alarmed by the widespread and knee-jerk reliance on pharmaceuticals by educators, who do not always explore fully the other options available for dealing with

---

*A version of this chapter first appeared in Salon.com, September 25, 2000.

learning and behavioral problems in their classrooms. Issues of medicine aside, these cases represent a direct challenge to the rights of parents to make choices for their children and still enjoy access to the public education they want for them—without medication. These policies also demonstrate a disquieting belief on the part of educated adults that bad behavior and underperformance in school should be interpreted as medical disorders that must be treated with drugs.

Unfortunately, I know from the experience of evaluating and treating more than 2,500 children for problems of behavior and school performance that these cases represent only a handful of the millions of Americans who have received pressure from school personnel to seek a medical evaluation for a child—teacher-speak for "get your kid on Ritalin."

Most often, evaluations are driven by genuine concerns first raised by a teacher or school psychologist. But too frequently the children are sent to me without even a cursory educational screening for learning problems. With a 1,700 percent increase in the use of Ritalin since 1990,[2] parents have been repeatedly told that their kids probably have ADHD and that Ritalin is the treatment of choice. More and more often, the parents who buck this trend are being told they must put their children in special restricted classrooms or teach them at home.

Patrick and Sarah McCormack (not their real names) came to my office in a panic last year because a school wanted them to medicate their seven-year-old son. Sarah tearfully explained that the principal and psychologist at Sammy's school in an upscale Bay Area town were absolutely clear that the first-grader should be on Ritalin. An outside private psychologist who had previously tested Sammy did not find any learning problems but concluded that he had ADHD and was defiant of authority. She suggested medication. The school psychologist, in his report on Sammy, was straightforward in recommending psychopharmacological therapy for the child.

The McCormacks were told, in no uncertain terms, that unless Sammy's behavior changed, he would be transferred to a special class for behavior-problem children at another school, or the McCormacks would have to consider alternatives to public education, such as home schooling.

Patrick and Sarah had few problems with their son at home, though they conceded he was a handful and sometimes had problems getting along with other children. They deeply valued his outgoing personality and feared that Ritalin would change him. They also worried about the immediate and long-term side effects of the drug. They acknowledged that Sammy struggled at school but felt school personnel had not done enough and were using the wrong approaches with their son. They hoped he could continue at the neighborhood school where he had made friends despite his problems. They wanted my opinion and support for their point of view at the school.

When I met Sammy in my office, he was full of life and reasonably focused, chatting at length about activities at home and at school. Though he was in first grade, he could read at a fourth-grade level. I got a better picture of his problems when I met him with his parents. When they were present, he acted impulsively, getting up and down from his seat and moving about the room when we tried to have a family conversation. Sammy regularly interrupted his parents and bossed them around, especially Sarah.

His lack of respect troubled me, but I felt optimistic that Sammy could be successful without medication, especially after I spoke with his teacher. She was more positive about him than others who had reported on his conduct at school. She felt he had made progress in her classroom but still wondered how she could help him stay on task better. She was open to ideas. I suggested that Sammy be immediately rewarded for good behavior and given chips for finished work that could be exchanged for prizes at the end of the day. She was comfortable with giving him tangible consequences, such as a time-out, for not meeting her expectations.

I suspected that medication would probably help with Sammy's self-control, but as I told the McCormacks, it was not absolutely necessary. I told them that children of Sammy's age never become addicted and that the drug's effects on his behavior would last only four hours per dose. But it was more important that they work on their parenting, and because of their distance from my office, I referred them to a local counselor. I couldn't say for sure whether changes at home and school would make the difference for Sammy, but I certainly felt it was up to the parents to decide on the medication. I said I would support their decision either way.

A year later, the McCormacks returned, frustrated and embittered. Sammy had had a very good end to first grade, but second grade, with an unsympathetic, unyielding teacher, had been disastrous. The principal and school district were now insisting that Sammy be on medication if he was to stay in a regular third-grade classroom. The school said it could not meet the child's needs within the regular classroom setting without medication. He was disrupting the classroom. Other parents had complained about his behavior. A one-on-one aide assigned to Sammy had not worked. Sarah thought the aide was nothing more than a snitch who regularly recorded Sammy's misdeeds for the principal.

If the family refused to give Sammy medication, the boy would be transferred to a different school, a bus ride from their home, to be in a special class with four other "disturbed" children. They could also home-school him or challenge the school's decision in a hearing. Ultimately they could go to court, but a final decision could take years— by then, Sammy might be in middle school. The parents were loath to move Sammy to a new school. However, they still were against using medication with their son.

Families such as the McCormacks, who reject medication and face a loss of access to conventional public school classrooms, are increasing in numbers. In May of 2000, I testified before a congressional subcommittee in a hearing on ADHD and Ritalin organized by several congressmen who had received letters from distressed parents pressured by their local schools to medicate their children. The pressure has become so intense that resolutions urging teachers to refrain from recommending medical evaluations and Ritalin for students have passed in more than a dozen states.

Yet even as the issue of parents' rights is being addressed in some areas, the stakes have dramatically increased in other areas, where schools are seeking the intervention of CPS to get parents to medicate their kids. It is no longer simply an issue of which school or which class a child will attend. Instead, some parents are being threatened with the possibility of losing custody of their children if they refuse to comply with suggested treatment for an alleged medical condition.

Many doctors and educators would agree that withholding medication can be viewed as a form of child abuse or neglect. In August 2001 Dr. Harold Koplewicz, vice chairman of the New York University Child Study Center, said on *Good Morning America* that he felt a CPS referral was justified when a family refused to medicate a child for whom a diagnosis of ADHD had been made by an experienced evaluator. Ritalin is simply the best treatment for this disorder, he said.

I can't agree. It is true that the courts have ordered medical intervention when a child's life is threatened. Judges have overruled the wishes of Christian Scientist parents not to give antibiotics to children who face life-threatening infection. Similarly, blood products have been given to children in surgery over the objections of Jehovah's Witnesses. But those situations are quite different from ones in which ADHD is diagnosed and Ritalin is prescribed, according to Dolores Sargent, a former special education teacher now practicing family law in Danville, California.

ADHD children and families do not face immediate life-threatening situations, she says, and ADHD continues to be a "disease" with multiple causes and no definitive markers. It's unlikely any decision that insists on the use of Ritalin for ADHD could withstand a court challenge.

The existence of effective alternative treatments makes any forced decision to medicate children against parents' wishes both legally and ethically shaky. Yet the willingness of some CPS workers to pursue families unwilling to dose their children shows how strongly entrenched medication for behavior problems in children has become in our country.

A local CPS office cannot demand that a child be medicated—not yet, anyway—but it can ascertain whether a child is safe in his or her parents' home. Legally, CPS can alert parents that their child's uncontrollable behavior, which puts the child at significant risk of abuse at home, must change. If CPS feels that this advice is not being taken, the agency can remove children from their homes.

What seems to be overlooked in this simplistic, and seemingly convenient, way of dealing with hard-to-handle kids is that alternative strategies to medication exist, from family counseling to short-term respite care. The perceived superiority, rapid onset, and inexpensive nature of Ritalin make it a very attractive choice for school administrators and teachers, who may pressure parents of students who threaten to drain their beleaguered schools of time or money. As more and more families opt for the Ritalin fix, it becomes easier to insist that other families in similar situations try the drug, even though these families may not want their kids to take stimulants.

I continue to prescribe Ritalin, but only after assessing a child's learning environment at school and family dynamics, especially the parents' style of discipline. But I persist in asking questions about Ritalin in a country where we use 80 percent of the world's stimulants.[3] I have no doubt that Ritalin works to improve short-term behavior and school performance in children with ADHD; however, it is not an equivalent to or a substitute for better parenting and schools for our children.

After much agonizing, Sammy's parents decided to put him in a special education class rather than give him Ritalin, and for the moment, things are going well for him. But they plan to move from the Bay Area, largely because of Sammy's school experience.

With four million children taking Ritalin in America today, there are undoubtedly millions of other parents struggling with the decision of whether to medicate their children. The McCormacks' story demonstrates the dilemmas and pressures many of these families face. Proponents of drug treatment for children's behavior problems applaud those parents who choose Ritalin to improve their children's

learning experience. But civil libertarians—and doctors like me—
worry about the specter of more families being forced against their
will to put their children on psychiatric medication. These families,
and their right to make choices for their children, deserve our support
and protection.

POSTSCRIPT—OCTOBER 2005

The McCormack family remained in touch with me over the subsequent years. Indeed, in the very conservative southwestern community they moved to, the pressures became so intense that the family
finally agreed to put Sammy on medication. The results were mixed.
Sammy's behavior improved some, but he continued to struggle—
because of, I suspect, his persistent oppositional, testing-the-limits
behavior. The family moved again, in 2003, this time to a small New
England town where there seemed to be more tolerance for different
kids. Perhaps it was also a factor that Sammy was getting older. He
continues on medication, and his overall coping seems better according to a recent email from Sarah.

In the meantime, elected officials have responded to parents' com-
plaints. In nineteen states there are laws on the books prohibiting
schools from mentioning ADHD or Ritalin in their reports to parents.
These "gag" laws strike me as a crude cudgel to stop the pressure. It
also prevents schools from appropriately alerting parents about real
consequences of the hyperactivity and impulsivity associated with
ADHD and the availability of an effective treatment, Ritalin. In my
experience, schools have learned how to communicate their concerns
to parents without using the specific label of ADHD.

More importantly, in the 2004 reauthorization of the Individuals
with Disabilities Education Act (IDEA), the principal federal law governing the rules and regulations of special education services in the
public schools, an amendment was introduced and passed prohibiting
public schools from denying children access to a classroom education
based upon families' refusal to use Ritalin-type drugs with their children.[4] Within the rules of the amendment there remains a great deal of
"wriggle room" for public school administrators to still offer very limited choices to recalcitrant parents who don't want to use medication
for their children. Still, the message to the schools from Congress
and the public is clear: back off from pressuring us to medicate
our children.[5]

On the other hand, controversy is growing over recommendations
for a broad-based public mental health screening of children and teenagers at school. The President's New Freedom Commission (a
name George Orwell, author of *1984*, could have proposed himself)

proposed Teen Screen to identify students who are at risk for mental illness via very simple questionnaires in school.[6] Questions such as "Have you ever thought of killing yourself?", "Have you felt depressed for more than two weeks at any time?" or "Do you have trouble falling or staying asleep?" are meant to screen children for further identification and potential treatment.

The appeal for screening children in school has multiple reasons. First, you have a captive audience. All children must attend school, or some equivalent, until the age of sixteen in most states. Second, proponents regularly bring up high rates of supposed undiagnosed and untreated mental illness in children and, in teenagers, high rates of suicide and suicide attempts. But prevalence data on mental illnesses (i.e., how prevalent a disorder appears to be) in general has become suspect. Indeed, most recent surveys show that up to half of all adults have a mental disorder at one point in their life, most beginning in late adolescence.[7] These surveys have been criticized as having far too broad criteria[8] but still are regularly invoked by psychiatric public health advocates as evidence for serious underidentification and undertreatment of mental illness, especially as a way of preventing more serious disease.

However, critics of these screening programs (an odd mix of civil libertarians, right-wingers, and Christian fundamentalists) fear earlier and finer identification will simply mean a further medicalization of the normal ups and downs of children, a further pathologizing of normal coping. They also worry that mental health diagnoses, these days, inevitably entail more drugging of children with psychiatric medications.

Unless positive screening leads first to a further examination of these children's lives, which inevitably will bring up family, social, and economic issues, I am reluctantly against these screening programs also. As long as the medical model of mental illness continues its reign in America, I fear mental health screening programs for children (strongly supported, not surprisingly, by the drug industry) will continue to ignore the broad public health challenges raised by these programs and instead focus on the individual for treatment. Given our priorities and limited resources in changing our children's lives, that treatment will likely be a drug.

7

Ritalin Works! Great?

"Annie's grades and behavior have improved so much that she no longer qualifies for special education," the school psychologist announced decisively. I was attending nine-year-old Annie's annual Individualized Educational Plan (IEP) review at her school as her behavioral pediatrician. The school psychologist sounded congratulatory, almost triumphant. Wasn't Annie an example of the goal of special education—to return a child to as normal a class setting as possible? Why then was I so uneasy about the school's decision to no longer provide services to this girl? As I left the school grounds, I shuddered while pondering the national implications of little Annie's "triumph."

As recently as three months ago, third-grader Annie was struggling with distractibility and inattention in her classroom. Getting her homework done and turned in on time was a nightly two-hour monumental effort on the part of her single-parent mother, Gail. Daily temper tantrums over rules and chores were also part of Annie's behavioral repertoire. Before coming to see me, Annie had been identified as learning disabled by the school in the first grade and had been enrolled in a special education program. Annie's pediatrician started her on Concerta, a long-acting version of the better-known stimulant drug Ritalin, for attention-deficit/hyperactivity disorder (ADHD), inattentive type.

Despite the confusion caused by its name, this kind of ADHD does not include hyperactivity or even much impulsivity, two of the three cardinal symptoms of ADHD. Simply the child must appear inattentive, distractible, and disorganized with poor task completion.

Virtually all children with inattentive ADHD have learning or processing problems, and their cognition has been described as "sluggish."

I coached Gail to respond to Annie much more quickly at home
with rewards and punishments. I suggested to Annie's teacher that
she handle Annie in a similar fashion. I also doubled Annie's medication dose for school. Annie responded beautifully, and within three
months the school was ready to eliminate her tutoring and behavioral
plan. So why was I unhappy?

Everyone in the room, including Annie's mother and me, believed
increasing Annie's medication was the single intervention that was
making the difference so quickly. Study after study has demonstrated
that stimulants such as Ritalin, Concerta, and Adderall improve, on
the short term, the performance and behavior of ADHD children. I
was certain that if Annie stopped the medication, most of her problems would return—I doubted she could have changed that quickly
solely with the behavioral program.

But with the medication improving Annie's performance, the
school was no longer obligated to provide services to Annie, as the
law was interpreted by school district's attorneys. In 1999, in *Sutton v.
United Airlines*, the U.S. Supreme Court ruled that when persons with
the use of mitigating measures are no longer functionally disabled,
they then no longer qualify for services under the American with Disabilities Act. Thus, for example, if glasses can correct a visual impairment, then the individual no longer is eligible for services.

John N. Hartson, a pediatric psychologist, is the national consultant to the American College of Testing Program for students with
ADHD requesting accommodations or services for disabilities. His
interpretation of the law goes beyond even this school district's policies.[1] If Dr. Hartson's suggestions were followed, Annie might never
have received any special education from her school in the first place.

Dr. Hartson believes, under his interpretation of federal guidelines coming from these court decisions, that if a school psychologist
diagnoses ADHD along with co-occurring problems (such as a learning disability or processing disorder), the child should first be given
a trial of Ritalin or its equivalent before any services for that child are
proposed by the school. Hartson expands on the Ritalin–glasses analogy with the following straw man case report to illustrate the question "Why offer services when glasses will correct all the problems?":

A child presents at an optometrists' office and is evaluated for
visual problems. The child is diagnosed with a problem with visual
acuity and the doctor suggests that the child be prescribed glasses.
The optometrist then sends the child to an educational specialist
who evaluates the child. The educational specialist sees the child

without glasses and notes that the child has a great deal of difficulty with reading and with correctly seeing items on a page. A number of recommendations are then offered including the need for preferential seating, larger print books . . . and additional time to complete reading and other visual tasks.[2]

Following Dr. Hartson's analogy, if a child like Annie with learning problems and ADHD demonstrates few or no problems in the classroom while on medication, then she should receive no services from the school. Only if she continued to have problems while on medication should she then be retested and offered appropriate educational services and accommodations. To offer services first or even simultaneously with medication is not consistent with federal guidelines according to Dr. Hartson.

But if we consider *all* federal guidelines, I'm confused. It would appear, given the interpretation of Annie's school district and Dr. Hartson, that a school could deny services and accommodations to a child with ADHD if the child was not first medicated. Yet Congress, reacting to perceived school pressure on families to medicate their children, added an amendment to the most recent authorization of the Individuals with Disability Education Act (IDEA) of 2004 that specifically prohibits schools from insisting that a child be medicated in order to attend classes in that district.

I'm not sure in the end how the government and the courts will reconcile what appears to be a conflict in "federal guidelines." In the short run, though, I suspect more and more school districts will try the medication-first approach and reconsider only if there is resistance from the family.

Dr. Hartson and others make an analogy between glasses for visual acuity and medication for ADHD. But is Ritalin the same as glasses? Apparently school districts continually looking to save money think so. Therefore, even inexpensive behavioral interventions, such as preferential seating in the front of the class, use of contingency rewards (e.g., stars, stickers, M&M's), and discipline contracts that have been shown to improve ADHD children's behavior and reduce the necessary dosage and frequency of medication, will not be offered if the medication alone "works."

In many children with the symptoms of ADHD (especially the inattentive type) who also have learning problems, who's to say which problem came first or what is causing what? In other words, might the learning or processing problems be contributing to the child's inattention and distractibility? Could addressing the educational needs of the child first without medication reduce or eliminate the need for drugs?

Furthermore, there's no evidence that just medication makes a difference in the *long-term* outcome of ADHD or learning problems. Ritalin teaches a child nothing. ADHD children "learn" to improve their behavior with appropriate behavioral and educational interventions. Yet the pressure on parents coming from schools to medicate their children will only grow when school districts look for legal ways to save money.

Dr. Hartson, like many other ADHD experts, considers two different types of interventions, medical interventions and nondrug interventions, equivalent if they both "work." However, the two types of interventions are not *morally* equivalent.[3] The best way to make clear this error, called a "logical fallacy of the means," is to also use an analogy, this one, literary. In the eighteenth century, the famous satirist Jonathan Swift wrote an essay entitled "A Modest Proposal." In it he offers a "solution" to the Irish potato famine crisis by suggesting Irish children be fed to their parents, providing nutrition while simultaneously decreasing the number of mouths to feed in one stroke.[4]

My "modest proposal" goes as follows. Currently about four million children take Ritalin or its equivalent, and classroom size averages about twenty-nine children per class. It is well know that Ritalin improves the performance of children with ADHD, with borderline ADHD, or even without ADHD. I propose we increase the number of children taking Ritalin to seven million. We could do this by continuing to broaden the criteria for ADHD (a process that's already been going on for fifteen years). Perhaps any child who performs below the median in a class might be referred for an ADHD evaluation and medication?

In any case, by increasing the number of children taking medication to seven million, we could enlarge class size to forty children, hire fewer teachers, and save school districts and tax payers a bundle of money. If, indeed, the medication–glasses analogy is valid and medication is the same as addressing the individual educational needs of children, there should be many educators and politicians ready to support my "modest proposal."

No takers? I wonder why not—because in a way we already substitute medication for nondrug services at school (in the cases of Annie and thousands of children like her). Until we are clear that a child's success while on Ritalin is not morally equivalent to a child's success with educational support, my proposal has a chance. But in all seriousness, we need to take a closer look at our priorities, the moral implications of our policies, and the way we determine which children get what help at school and at home.

8

Getting Up to Speed
for the SAT

American children are taking stimulants and other psychiatric drugs at an unprecedented rate.[1] The reasons for this phenomenon are complex and widespread.[2] But stories that I've been hearing for years and that are now confirmed by research data illuminate at least one part of the answer. My first clue came in 2002, when a television news producer called me about a Manhattan doctor who was giving her high school son Ritalin before important exams. She asked me if I had ever heard of such a practice. I had not, but I wasn't shocked. It seemed rather inevitable that parents would use Ritalin that way to boost their kids' performance.

Indeed, about six months later, I too directly received a telephone call from a psychiatrist parent who asked me if I would consider medicating her teenager son just for exam taking. He had previously tried Concerta and found that it cut down on his "sociability" and wanted to take it just for exams. She could write the prescriptions herself, but she thought it would be better if her son was managed by someone other than his mother. I knew I would never agree to such a plan, but I was intrigued. I suggested that she, her husband, and her son come in, but I never heard back from them.

People are still surprised to learn that Ritalin, Adderall, and Concerta, along with all the other new stimulant drug formulations prescribed ostensibly to treat ADHD, also work in "normal" children and adults. A myth continues, which began with the very first case reports in the 1930s, that stimulants work "paradoxically" to calm hyperactive children.[3] In reality, stimulant drugs have the same effect on everybody—low doses (such as those for ADHD) improve everyone's concentration and get people to be more methodical. The hyperactivity of ADHD decreases because the kids stick longer with tasks that used to bore them quickly.

Experts have known about the universal enhancing effects of the stimulants for years. The army explored the routine use of stimulants on GIs in the 1950s. (The Allies widely distributed amphetamine to soldiers in World War II after learning that the German general Rommel was giving stimulants to his famed Afrika Corps.) Although stimulants regularly improved the soldiers' alertness and performance on boring tasks, there were enough episodes of "erratic" behavior that the generals decided that giving amphetamine routinely to guys with guns was not a good idea.[4]

In the late 1970s, the National Institute of Mental Health (NIMH) proved irrefutably that stimulants improve the performance of normal men and boys as much as they do for those with ADHD.[5] College students have also known about the performance-enhancing effects of Ritalin, and since the 1990s boom in ADHD diagnosis, prescription stimulants have been freely traded or sold on campus, often crushed and snorted, for "power" studying or to get high.[6] Recent reports have up to one in four students on some college campuses using prescription stimulants illegally.[7] A specter of misuse of, tolerance of, and addiction to prescription stimulants hangs over such use.

But I was not especially surprised by these stories I'd heard or by the call I received about Ritalin being considered for children just to improve performance on tests. Of course, that mother-physician was acting unethically when prescribing the drug to her own son. Regardless of the ethics of performance enhancement, treating members of your own family for any reason is considered a "no-no" in all of medicine.

But what *is* disturbing is that many kids are probably getting stimulants from their doctors for alleged ADHD (or are taking them on their own) and using them just "as needed." This isn't necessarily because doctors are bad or lousy diagnosticians. Teenage and adult ADHD, except in extreme cases, is actually difficult to delineate. The line between the unmotivated or learning impaired and those with ADHD is very much in the eye of the beholder. Doctors already routinely prescribe stimulants like Ritalin or Adderall "just for school." Several of my college-age patients take Concerta only three days a week—on the days they have classes. They say they don't need the drug otherwise.

I draw the line though with people who want the drug only for occasional use—even if they meet my criteria for ADHD. Such intermittent use enables the procrastination and last minute panic typical of an ADHD lifestyle. But Ritalin for the ADHD diagnosis is a slippery slope, and many of the kids getting Ritalin from their doctors look pretty normal to me. Still they will do "better than normal" on Ritalin.

Unlike young children who never become addicted, teens and adults do run the risk of abuse, tolerance, and addiction with prescription stimulants. Just recently, in February of 2006, I received phone calls within two weeks of each other from parents who had discovered that their teenagers were abusing Adderall. (I predict we will ultimately learn that Adderall and Adderall XR are the prescription stimulant drugs most abused by teens and young adults in comparison with Ritalin or Concerta. That's because Adderall is amphetamine, and the other two are methylphenidate-based. And although the two chemicals are very similar, I feel that amphetamine is the more intense experience, even when used therapeutically, and therefore it will attract the greater number of abusers.)

One of these kids, a seventeen-year-old senior at the local high school told his mother that he had taken "a hit" of Adderall just before taking the SAT exam. He thought it was very helpful, and indeed he received a perfect 800 in the verbal part of the three-part exam. He had always "underperformed" in school according to his mother, and now both she and her son were interested in his trying the drug on a more regular basis. Unfortunately, as I learned more about this boy— his daily marijuana use, his selling it at school, and the general chaos of his home life—I knew that neither he nor his mother had the organizational responsibility necessary to safely handle a drug with the abuse potential of Adderall (or Concerta for that matter).

These individual stories of illegal use and abuse of prescription stimulants and the many more anecdotes reported nationally were finally confirmed by a statistical study of misuse of these drugs that appeared in the journal *Drug and Alcohol Dependence* in early 2006.[8] The authors analyzed government-collected data of face-to-face interviews with 54,000 people in 2002. Taking into account U.S. 2000 census data, the researchers estimated that over seven million people have misused prescription stimulants. Of children between twelve and seventeen years old, 2.6 percent reported misusing stimulants, and in the age group of eighteen to twenty-five, 5.9 percent admitted to illegal prescription stimulant use.

More sobering are the stories of those younger kids who acknowledged use of these drugs and who met *DSM-IV* criteria for drug dependency or drug abuse. A little more than one in ten children who begin with casual use of these drugs go on to become stimulant addicts. This translates to about 75,000 teens and young adults in 2002 addicted to prescription stimulants. And annual production quota rates from the Drug Enforcement Administration (DEA) indicate that more legal speed has been produced in our country since that time.[9]

A couple of doctors like me and officials from the Chemical Diversion Division of the DEA have fretted for years about the likelihood of a fourth wave of doctor-prescribed stimulant abuse. I earlier mentioned the Allies' use of these drugs with American GIs during World War II. Many of these soldiers came back to the States addicted to amphetamine. The early 1960s were marked by an era of "Dr. Feelgoods" who went so far as to inject amphetamine intravenously into their patients for a variety of ill-defined medical and emotional problems. The last wave of doctor-prescribed stimulant abuse (until this current one) took place in the 1970s and only ended when Congress and the states set limits and penalties on the use of prescription amphetamine for weight loss and control. [10]

Repeatedly, American doctors and American society seem to lose their collective memory over these drugs and find another reason to prescribe them. "America Taking 'Uppers'," legal or illegal, ran a headline of a UN Narcotic Control Report in 1999.[11] These drugs "work," no doubt, but at least in adults, whether they are used for losing weight or concentrating better, the evidence is only for short-term benefits. When the long-term data on weight loss and stimulants was examined by doctors and public officials in the 1970s, it was clear that in the long term, the medications were ineffective, and development of tolerance (needing increasing doses for the same effect) was common.[12]

The longest study on the effects of prescription stimulants among teens and adults ran only two to three months. There are no long-term studies of, say, five years. In my experience of treating about fifteen older teens and adults for over five years, I'd estimate that in only three or four cases has the drug really made a difference in the quality of their lives (e.g., improved their employment status or family life). Ominously, tolerance has developed in four of these patients (my limit with them is 90 mg of Adderall XR daily).

The downside of prescription stimulants has been well known to researchers for decades, but for example, as of early 2006, I had still not found one research article on the development of tolerance with the use of prescription stimulants in adults. To some extent, doctors and the public have been misled by the excellent safety record of the use of these drugs in the preteen population. No child under thirteen has ever been reported to be addicted to Ritalin. Children don't have access to the medication and interestingly don't like higher doses ("I feel nervous. I feel weird," is what they tell their parents when the dose gets too high for them.). But access to the medication and response to higher doses ("I feel powerful. I feel grand.") are different in older teens and adults.

Ironically, the first study that analyzed the government data on prescription stimulant abuse was funded by Eli Lilly, the makers of Strattera, the only nonstimulant, non-abusable drug approved for the treatment of ADHD. Lilly's strategy is obvious. Lilly hopes this study will raise further concerns about drugs such as Adderall and Concerta that clearly work better than Strattera for ADHD but that have abuse potential. It seems in America that if there isn't money to be made, no one will do the work necessary to find out if any drug is safe or works long-term.

But in fact, most people can use prescription stimulants occasionally without much trouble. As word of the "benefits" of these drugs continues to spread, we will hear more about the use of Ritalin (and the other prescription stimulants) in questionable situations. In sports competition, the use of performance enhancing drugs is banned. In athletics we value not just the performance itself but also the effort involved in the achievement. Taking a drug somehow cheapens that performance.

These drugs are also banned because if we permit one athlete to take performance drugs, then we actually put pressure on all the other competing athletes to take the drug too, just in order to stay even. My seventeen-year-old son, a junior in high school, tells me about rampant Adderall use at his school during exam time for studying or test taking. We've talked about it at home and agree that improved performance by taking a drug isn't worth the improvement or the risk, but I still wonder if he isn't feeling some pressure to take these drugs too.

But isn't school different from sports anyway? Well, yes and no, yet there's certainly a competitive element to academics, especially with exams like the SAT, GREs, MCATs, and LSATs. Without a clear line for diagnosis, how do we really know who legitimately "has or doesn't have" ADHD and who can benefit from Ritalin? And with so much available prescription stimulant medication out there anyway, you don't really need to go to a doctor to get your pills for the test.

It sounds incredible at this moment to consider, but will we in the near future need to require students to submit to random drug urine testing before they take important exams? Our national obsession with performance continues, and Ritalin will only complicate the race. But ultimately, a society that chooses to cope with life's challenges by turning to drugs does so at its own peril.

9

The Invariant Prescription Redux: The Key to Effective Parenting[*]

In the early 1980s, as an impressionable young family therapist, I remember picking up a copy of the Italian analyst-turned-family therapist Mara Selvini Palazzoli's *Paradox and Counterparadox*.[1] After reading the book in two days, I became a convert and carried it with me to every family therapy session I attended. I was floored—here was an elegant and precise approach for such difficult and often intractable problems as anorexia and schizophrenia. As the whole field of family therapy seemed galvanized with Palazzoli's methods, I became one of the few behavioral pediatricians who began to work using a one-way mirror with a team of therapists who issued bold interventions to my most difficult cases.

But in the mid-1980s, Palazzoli announced that she had abandoned her earlier paradoxical approach and shocked and confused her most admiring devotees with her book *Family Games*,[2] in which she set forth her "invariant prescription." Her new book revealed the details of a seemingly simple but deceivingly complex intervention that she employed for all of her cases, which were mostly the families of seriously disturbed teenagers. She had the parents secretly plan to and

---

[*]A version of this chapter appeared in *Family Therapy Networker*, 2000.

then spend at least one night away from their home and their problem offspring, without preparing the child or explaining their actions.

That was it. Palazzoli claimed that once the parents took such an action, the teenager's problems, regardless of their nature, would diminish. I remember reading *Family Games* with increasing skepticism and disappointment. How could the great Palazzoli have become so simple-minded and reductionistic? After all, the idea that there was a single solution to all teenage problems seemed utterly absurd. But I trusted and believed so much in Palazzoli that, despite my misgivings, I tried to apply her new intervention on several occasions, without much success. I realized then as now that this prescription was not as simple as it appeared. It directly addressed overprotection, enmeshment, triangulation, anxiety, guilt, and poor limits—the core of the problems between these parents and adolescents. "Selling" or reframing the action for parents was the great challenge. I was never entirely successful in my efforts, but even the conversations I had about the intervention with the parents who struggled with their teens were revealing and sometimes productive.

A few years before Palazzoli announced her invariant prescription, Jay Haley, another major figure of family therapy, made a similar stab at a one-size-fits-all solution. In *Leaving Home*, he argued that the key to treating families with intractable teenagers was to restore the power of parents at virtually any cost.[3] Then and only then would an adolescent's behavior and functioning improve. There was nothing especially clever about some of the heavy-handed techniques he proposed for increasing parents' leverage, which could involve calling the police or kicking the kid out of the house. Haley, like Palazzoli, was also widely dismissed as having become too obsessed with hierarchy and power.

I have now had a practice of behavioral pediatrics and family therapy for more than twenty-five years in an affluent suburb of the San Francisco Bay Area. I've seen my share of depressed children and adolescents who are suicidal at times or even psychotic. More common and nearly epidemic, though, are acting out preschool age to high school boys who could meet the criteria for attention-deficit/hyperactivity disorder (ADHD), oppositional defiant disorder (ODD), or both. Although more and more girls present these days with the acting-out problems of ADHD or ODD, more typically I see the girls for the problems of fears, phobias, anxiety, or depression. Obsessive-compulsive disorder (OCD), learning disorders, and relational-communication disorders such as autism or Asperger's syndrome round out my fare.

Having evaluated and treated about 2,500 children and their families, I've concluded that over the years I have adhered to one guiding principle with all the families I see. My proposal, like those of Palazzoli and Haley, may generate some ridicule and dismissal, but I feel compelled to share it nevertheless: children's behavior and emotions improve when parents become more effective in their discipline and limit setting.

The key to clinical effectiveness shouldn't be that simple or reductionistic or so generalized, yet over and over again, I have seen that once parents become effective executives, the children do better. And it's not just with the acting-out problems of ADHD, ODD, or conduct disorder that this improvement occurs. Even children with anxiety or OCD get better.

It has gotten to the point that my belief in the importance of discipline borders on an "invariant prescription" for children's problems. Of course, it's hardly earth-shattering news that discipline and limits are important for healthy children. Yet, in the rush to medicalize children's problems and prescribe the right pill for every occasion, the ubiquity of the need for discipline has become overlooked.

Susan and Bill Cash weren't sure they had a problem with their six-year-old, Ryan. The parents were a highly educated, thoughtful, self-confident couple in their mid-thirties. They weren't having many problems dealing with Ryan at home, but the staff at South River Academy, a private Christian school where Ryan attended the first grade, called Susan regularly. "He's having trouble conforming to their discipline requirements," Susan said. I asked them for more details. "They say he's up and down from his seat. He tends to do what he wants. He's not responding to their reward system for behavior. Once he gets involved in a project, he has no problems completing it. It just may be hard to get him to stop if the rest of the class is doing something else." The parents weren't certain whether his behavior was all that unusual for a six-year-old boy. But they were concerned with the teachers' reports, which had mentioned getting a medical evaluation for ADHD.

I met Ryan next with his parents and sister. He and his four-year-old sister, Casey, rushed in ahead of their parents. Both children headed for the bins of toys on a table in the far corner of the room. I asked the parents if the children could first join us on the couch. Bill's first request failed. They came when Susan called them over. Ryan was the size of an average six-year-old, but his sturdy body seemed to move constantly, even when he was seated on the couch or floor.

I was dubious about being able to engage the children in a long conversation, so I asked Susan and Bill to perform a short puppet play about a kid who was having some trouble in a classroom. Ryan interrupted his parents regularly and tried to wander away back to the toys, stopping only when intercepted by his mother. He followed the

story his parents portrayed well enough, and when Fred, the designated puppet child, hadn't followed the puppet teacher's instructions,
Ryan shouted, "Give him a time-out!"

The story ended and I announced a period of "free-play" with the
toys. The kids grabbed puppets of their own, and I noticed that Ryan's
main efforts were directed at hitting and biting his mother's puppet.
Susan, with increasing exasperation, valiantly attempted to redirect
Ryan's aggressive actions toward something more socially acceptable,
but was unsuccessful. It worried me that Ryan seemed to so relish
hurting and inflicting pain on another, even in play.

My meeting with the Cash family left me feeling that things weren't
as easy at home as the parents suggested. Both these kids were intense
and determined, and I wondered whether Ryan was inherently hyperactive. A call to his first-grade teacher reinforced my concerns. Mrs. Gray
had no doubts about Ryan's academic abilities. But she had to pay attention to him constantly; otherwise he would break from what he was
doing to sharpen his pencil, go to the computer, or bother one of his
tablemates. She said that none of his classmates wanted to sit next to him.

I inquired about her methods for reinforcing behavior and discipline. The school's policy was to emphasize positive behavior with
verbal praise. They did not feel comfortable using any tangible
rewards, such as stickers, for the kids. On occasion, when all else
failed, Ryan would be sent to the back of the room for a time-out or,
rarely, out of the classroom to the office. I asked Mrs. Gray how much
she thought Ryan could control his behavior. "Oh, I don't think he can
at all," she said, adding that although she wasn't a doctor, she had
"had other kids like Ryan who turned out to be ADD."

I met with Susan and Bill alone after the family's visit. They were
anxious to hear my thoughts about Ryan and the family. I presented a
picture of Ryan's temperament as intense, determined, and mildly
impulsive. I said that many doctors would be ready to diagnose Ryan
as ADHD and prescribe Ritalin. I knew that the Cashes were not eager
to put Ryan on medication and were ready to try anything to help their
son, especially at school. I said that I thought there was a possibility
of avoiding medication if they were willing to work on their discipline.

Actually, I did not know how much Ryan might improve with
solid effective discipline from his parents and teacher, but I sensed an
ambivalence, in both the parents and the teacher, about setting limits,
which severely compromised the effectiveness of the approaches they
were currently using. Ryan was not bigger, stronger, or wiser than
they were. He was simply more determined, less ambivalent, and
more intense about his purpose. His caregivers, worried about damaging his self-esteem, were hoping to avoid conflict and remain posi-

tive. They tried to use the "talk to your kid so he will listen" approach, a variation of the title of a best-selling advice book to parents.

But this wasn't a cognitive question for Ryan. He knew the puppet, Fred, was doing the wrong thing. Try talking to Ryan, I thought, and he's halfway down the street before you've finished your first sentence. But despite this repeated experience, his parents persisted with too many words. Others might theorize differently. Today's biological psychiatrists and their legion of minions would opine "he can't self-regulate" because of a genetic predisposition to ADHD and chemical imbalance. Medication is the first, and probably the only, answer needed. But I wanted to know how Ryan would behave if his parents and teacher could be organized and consistent about more immediate and tangible rewards and punishments. By using the "p" word, I knew I was committing a mortal sin within the world of politically correct parenting, which is dedicated to protecting children's self-image at all costs. But I also knew from much experience that rewards alone would not work with the Ryans of America.

I'm not thinking about electric shock or even spanking (that's a whole other subject). Most of the time, parents and teachers simply must take action sooner—often the same actions they currently take, but only after repeated provocations. Repeated testing behavior makes most moms and dads angry. Only then can they can overcome their ambivalence about punishment and take effective actions.

However, every time Ryan ignores his parents' verbal repetitions without repercussions, their words become less effective. What can Susan and Bill do? This is not rocket science. Give Ryan only one warning and then remove the offending toy for an hour. Don't throw it away as parents often threaten when repeatedly frustrated. Withhold a privilege, such as dessert, if he doesn't sit at the dinner table without getting up for five minutes. Decline the goodnight hug if he refuses to put on his pajamas by 9:00 PM. Susan and Bill hold tremendous power over Ryan, but they feel uncomfortable about using it effectively. They talk too much.

To convince parents to try discipline with their children, I've found it helpful to explain the reason that children test the limits of their parents and why it is important that parents have control over their children's behavior: children feel emotionally more secure when they experience their parents as more powerful and consistent than themselves. I sometimes add that children recognize their dependency on their parents at a very early age, and when they experience themselves as "stronger" than their folks, kids feel emotionally insecure. Their behavior asks the question, "If I am too little to take care of myself, but I am stronger than they are, then who is taking care of me?"

There's a great deal of psychological literature that supports the effectiveness of discipline,[4] but simply from experience, I have seen children over and over again become more affectionate toward their parents after the initial battling is over and the parents' power has been affirmed. I used to think the children were just "kissing up"—they hoped that if they showed affection, the parents would relax and ease their discipline and punishments. Many parents do relax their rules—mostly because their children's behavior improves—and indeed, the children's affection disappears, and their negative testing behavior begins anew.

Discipline isn't everything, of course. We therapists all worry about the authoritarian parent—the cold, distant, harsh disciplinarian whose children can never do enough to please. But in my suburban practice, the authoritarian parent seems a vanishing species, truly on the verge of extinction. The average middle-class parent has become quite sophisticated about the importance of "expressing feelings." The authoritarian parent by nature is less likely to turn to therapy to solve a child problem in any case.

I am afraid that today's children who appear in therapists' offices don't have a problem with too little expression of feeling. The problem is they are usually expressing *too much* with captive parents who feel it is their job to understand and attempt to accept or tolerate their children's messages and behavior. There are exceptions. Emotional trauma in the form of physical and sexual abuse, neglect, marital conflict, and divorce continue to contribute to the behavior problems of children. These children benefit from a safe and neutral arena for their views and feelings. But too often, the process of therapy for these children is limited to just that. Limits are just as important for these children, perhaps even more so given that their basic sense of security and trust has been eroded or damaged.

Children absolutely need regular affection and the opportunity to make choices, too. Demonstrations of affection and caring—hugging, kissing, spending time with children on their level—make them feel validated and loved as individuals. It also makes them more cooperative when limits are set. Children should also be allowed to make choices. However, for the vast majority of children I see in my office, simple offers of love and choice do not work. These parents overwhelmingly love their children and show it. But their love is not enough. Solid discipline makes the children feel secure. I also remind parents that one cannot nurture and discipline simultaneously—the two acts effectively cancel each other out. Discipline is best done with some emotional distance. Nurture a child, but separate that from setting a limit.

The invariant prescription of solid discipline for children seems deceptively simple but is demanding on the family. If either parent or the marriage is in trouble, the consistency and immediacy of rewards and punishments necessary for effectiveness will be difficult to achieve. I call this the "oxygen mask theory of parenting." When flight attendants instruct passengers on the use of emergency equipment before air travel, they give special instructions about the use of the oxygen masks when sitting next to a young child who may need assistance. "First place the mask over your face, and then place a mask over the child." Otherwise, both parent and child may pass out.

Too many parents don't have enough oxygen flowing to themselves in their daily lives to effectively help their children. Depressed parents, overworked parents, substance-abusing parents, and parents with very unhappy marriages are not able to deliver effective discipline to their children. They lack consistent standards and follow-through. Sometimes, they'll ignore their children's testing behavior; other times, they'll overreact and then feel guilty afterward. The children experience a roller coaster of supervision and discipline that hardly satisfies their need for security.

However, problem children also stress parents and marriages. So, except in the most obvious cases of parental mental illness or marital dysfunction, I try to work on parenting first. Sometimes, the marriage improves overall when the parents can agree on and achieve some success with the children's problems. But other times, the parents' problems are simply too great and must be addressed first. In those cases, unless parental mental health and relationships improve, only Band-Aid therapy can be offered to the child.

Employing my invariant prescription with Susan and Bill, I offered the basic reframe of interpreting Ryan's problems as a repetitive unconscious behavioral attempt to ask the question, "Are you steady and strong enough to take care of me?" Ryan experienced Susan and Bill's efforts at comfort, placation, and explanation, though noble in intent, as weakness. Would they be willing to temporarily put aside their well-intentioned means to their goal of a harmonious loving family with a confident and happy son and employ strategies that would convince Ryan that they were more consistent and powerful than he could be?

The speed and intensity with which the parents, especially Susan, adopted this point of view surprised me. Apparently, she'd been thinking a great deal about their parenting style. She was raised more strictly herself and judged her childhood overall as positive. She had been confused by the contradictory advice offered by the school, her pediatrician, and the myriad self-help books on parenting when it came to discipline. Bill was also comfortable making a change.

They decided to work on having Ryan sit for five minutes at the dinner table and get ready in the morning for school without so much fussing and delay. They would use a timer at dinner to help Ryan monitor the time, and they were prepared to have him miss his meal and not eat anything else until morning if he failed to sit. He would get an extra helping of dessert when he successfully stayed seated for five minutes. We went over a procedure for an effective time-out for Ryan should he become too angry.

We also altered the morning routine. Susan and Bill told Ryan he must accomplish the few tasks he needed to do—get up, eat breakfast, brush his teeth, and comb his hair—before he'd be allowed to put on his clothes for school. They would give him three reminders of the time that was left before the family had to leave. Whether he dawdled or delayed was his choice, but any clothes not on him by the time they had to leave would be put in a shopping bag left near the front door, and he could get dressed at school. I told the parents to actually let him get dressed in the back seat of their car the first time, but not to tell him about this partial amnesty in advance.

Susan and Bill returned the next week, pleased and astonished at Ryan's improvements at dinner and in the mornings. Over the next three months, I saw them with the children four more times. I noticed immediately the change in Susan's words and tone of voice when she had to set a limit or offer a directive. Gone were the questions such as "Do you want to help clean up the toys?" Instead, with her voice deepening just a bit and her tone lowering at the end, she said "Help me clean up the toys now." Could nothing more remarkable than that lead to Ryan's improved cooperation and decreased activity in my office? It appears so. It turns out that, at heart, he was a pleaser.

Ryan's behavior also improved at school. Susan said she shared with Mrs. Gray how well immediate and tangible rewards were working to keep Ryan on task. His teacher then began offering Ryan "special pennies" that could be used for prizes and privileges at the end of the week. She found that giving immediate rewards worked so well with Ryan that she was offering the pennies to the entire class.

Ryan's experience is unusual in my practice only in that I believed the impulsive aspects of his personality were making things more difficult for him and his family. I was genuinely prepared to offer him Ritalin if the efforts of his parents and school failed to help him sufficiently. But as it turned out, Ryan, like so many other less intense children, succeeded after his caregivers made specific changes in their behavior toward him.

It's easy to see how effective discipline would apply to acting-out children, but when limits to rescuing are set for children with problems such as anxiety, phobia, or OCD, their symptoms and sense of well-being also rapidly improve.[5] Anna was an eleven-year-old girl whose fears were so upsetting that her mother, Joann, had not been able to leave her daughter's side for the previous three weeks during the summer vacation. Joann's employer was unwilling to have her bring Anna to work, so Joann hadn't gone in herself and was at risk of losing her job. The family met me in crisis over this emergency, having already been to another psychiatrist, who had started Anna on Prozac. Anna had taken the medication for two weeks without much change in her behavior.

Anna had always been a sensitive girl, but separations had never been a major problem before. She was a cute, blond-haired child who acted younger in her mother's presence than the usual preteen. The mother and daughter appeared "glued" to one another in my office as they spoke of a "chemical imbalance" that likely caused Anna's panic disorder.

I had little doubt that Anna's sensitivities and fears were out of control and making her more and more upset. She was now scared about being scared. Her mother's increasing desperation and panic undoubtedly also frightened her. In essence, both mother and daughter were in an out-of-control cycle. I knew if I could help Anna's mother feel comfortable about setting some limits over the discussion and power of Anna's fears, both she and Anna would improve.

With a nod to Michael White's narrative model,[6] I asked Anna and Joann if they could give a name to the powerful, irrational feeling that overtook Anna and turned a sensible and competent child into a helpless victim. They came up with the not especially original Mr. Fear. We then worked together on an "anxiety thermometer" for OCD, developed by John March, a child psychiatrist from Duke University.[7] We linked specific activities with their attendant feelings to "temperatures" from 98.6 (meaning she wasn't frightened) to increasing levels of temperature and fear. Being left at home with a sitter while her mother went to work was rated at 104 degrees.

We also reviewed "exceptions" to the problem—previous situations in which Mr. Fear had been in charge, but now no longer bothered Anna. All children learn to walk and have to overcome the fear of falling. Nearly all remember learning to ride a bicycle. Anna also had a specific fear of being locked in a bathroom and not being able to get out, which no longer bothered her. We went over how she had "gotten used to it" and how that could work with her current problem.

All this was done with Joann's participation because she was actually my main audience. I have learned that even the most desperate-to-change child improves more quickly when the parents provide prompts in the form of rewards and punishments to encourage the necessary exposure-desensitization experiences. Decreasing the parents' anxieties and worries about their child seems key to the abatement of the child's fear.

"If I cannot control my own thoughts and my mother cannot help me, then I surely am in big trouble" is how I began to reframe Anna's situation to Joann afterward, when we were alone. I spoke very carefully to Joann because she clearly felt Anna couldn't help herself. I agreed, telling Joann that Anna had an uncontrollable irrational fear that was running and ruining both their lives. I asked Joann if she'd be willing to help her daughter by not letting Anna's fears so completely rule her mother. At the very least, she might resist the power of Anna's fears by giving in less to Anna's demands.

Initially, Joann was supposed to not talk to Anna as much about Anna's problems. She was to tell Anna that it was okay to be upset, but when she felt that way, it was better to be in her room. Joann could then engage in some enticing activity, such as cooking, which Anna enjoyed, that would shift the focus away from the problem. I also instructed Joann to give Anna five minutes of "complaining time" during which Anna could "invite Mr. Fear in," but at the end of the five minutes, she had to "kick him out." Joann's job during the five minutes was to listen and appreciate Anna's concerns—not argue, reason, or suggest solutions. Once the five minutes were up, if she kept on complaining, Anna would again be asked to keep Mr. Fear company in her room.

Having made some changes in how they coped with Anna's anxiety, Joann decided to challenge the power of Anna's fear, with her daughter's reluctant consent, by leaving her with her grandmother and driving around the block for five or ten minutes. Anna would be rewarded with a dollar toward a special CD she wanted if she coped reasonably. This resulted in some protests and upset, but within days, Anna began to improve, and after a week, Joann was able to return to work. In an analogous hierarchical fashion, I set a limit (with Joann's assent) on Joann, and then she effectively set limits on her own anxiety and rescue behavior with Anna.

It's cruel to force someone with one short leg to run the race as fast as everyone else. No matter how much you punish or reward, that person will limp. But I sincerely believed in Anna's competence, as well as in her mother's. Joann believed that Anna was incapacitated by her brain chemistry, so she expected very little from her daughter; medication was the answer for this "broken brain." The handicaps of a separation anxiety are harder to define than those, say, of a shorter leg, but even wheelchair victims benefit from limits and expectations that hold them to their potential competencies. When parents proceed with sympathy but expect some competence from their children and follow through accordingly, their kids improve.

There has been much discussion over the success of cognitive–behavioral approaches and desensitization techniques for children with anxiety, phobias, and OCD. But these treatments work better when parents motivate their children with rewards and consequences for acting courageously. I'm not suggesting that we eliminate children from therapy sessions. (Haley suggested as much in his satiric essay "In Defense of Child Therapy".) They can be partners with their parents in developing a treatment plan. But therapy will be most effective when the parents, and to a lesser extent other caregivers in school and day care, are mobilized.

Even the depressed child benefits from limits. Depressed, anxious children improve with talk and support, but continued talk without any change in behavior actually tends to contribute to the problem. Limiting talk and decreasing the possibility of secondary gain, which are both forms of discipline, and offering enticements for activity and involvement are the ideal combinations for helping a child become "undepressed." That is, of course, assuming something can be done about the child's environment that contributed to the unhappiness in the first place.

Ironically, the proposition of discipline appears simple whereas families are complex. But a growing number of therapists working with children and their families agree that the simple application of consistent discipline and limit setting is the solution to a variety of complex family problems. The proposition that we are a hierarchical species and that children feel more comfortable when they know where they fit in the pecking order may not be politically correct and may even make some of us uncomfortable. But, ultimately, it makes sense biologically—parents must pass on vast quantities of information and life skills before their children can function on their own; that can be accomplished much more effectively in a natural order in which children are taught to listen.

We hear so much these days about ADHD, OCD, depression, and bipolar disorder—conditions that are felt to be hereditary, biological, and chronic. Ineffective psychotherapies directed at children are commonly offered in the early stages of these conditions. The failure of these therapies often leads to the conclusion that the child is mentally ill. So much unnecessary treatment and medication can be prevented if only therapists and physicians spend some time directing parents and schools to become more comfortable and effective with their discipline. That said, I know it's hardly as simple as it sounds, but that is where the complex area of family therapy begins.

10

In the Valley of Motivational Fatigue—Diagnosing ADHD in Early Adolescence

Fourteen-year-old Jack sits slump-shouldered in a chair in my office. His body language exudes boredom as we converse. He keeps the hood of his Oakland Raiders sweatshirt over his head regardless of the temperature in the room. His oversized pants hang so low that his boxer shorts show. Jack generally mumbles when he answers my queries about his experiences as an eighth-grader at his public middle school. I move my chair closer to him as I strain to make out his answers.

"I'm getting mostly Ds and Fs at this point," he says rather matter-of-factly. For all his struggles and posturing, Jack's pretty honest with me. "I don't always do my homework. Sometimes I forget to turn it in, so my grades suck—all my majors [major subjects] weigh homework big as part of my grade. See, I'm getting an A in music and computer. They don't give homework." He told me he always passes PE too.

According to Jack's mother, his reading abilities had always been slightly behind, starting as early as the first grade. His grades, nevertheless, were adequate and satisfactory to his parents until he began middle school. In the seventh grade, he managed to bring several Ds up to Bs and Cs at the end of the year, but only after his parents threatened him with "permanent grounding" unless he started doing his homework.

But this year, even with missing out on seeing his friends regularly because of parental restrictions on his weekend activities, Jack's efforts were minimal and his grades remained low. Last year, one of his seventh-grade teachers mentioned the nonhyperactive form of ADHD to his parents as a possible cause for Jack's poor school performance. Then, with the bottom falling out for Jack in the eighth grade, two of Jack's teachers reported that he was distractible, inattentive, and poorly organized. Jack agreed: "I try to get some of my homework done in the back of the room when the teacher is collecting it from everyone else. I know that's bad but I can't seem to get myself to do it until then."

Jack also endorsed the concentration problem. "I just can't concentrate when I try to do my work." He knew vaguely about ADHD and taking medication to do better in school. Two of his friends were on meds. He seemed sincere about his attentional woes. However, both he and his parents agreed that outside the arena of academics (whether at school or with homework), Jack generally had few problems. For example, he usually completed his chores at home with only two or three reminders, which didn't strike his parents as too unusual for a fourteen-year-old boy.

Jack sprang to life when we talked about his other interests: skateboarding and music. He took his skateboard everywhere—that's how he got to my office, actually.

"How high can you olly?" I asked, straining to remember the arcane skateboarding argot my sons had employed when they went through their skateboarding phase.

"About this high," he replied, his hand about a foot above the floor.

"Not bad," I commented. "Where do you grind?" I was actually less interested in learning the location where the skaters try to get the flat part of their boards to slide across a surface than in seeing if I could keep Jack engaged in our conversation. "Took a little while for you to get good at skating?" I asked innocently of Jack.

"Man, I dig it," Jack said. "I don't mind taking the time. I hang out with my friends. We kill a lot of time that way. I also get tired. It's work."

Jack's other interest was bass guitar. He had recently switched from experimenting with acoustic and lead guitars to playing the bass. He was serious about playing electric bass in a band that he and his friends had just formed. "It's tight," Jack said with enthusiasm about practicing with his new band. He told me he felt more comfortable playing bass than being out front with the lead guitar.

"You have a name for your band yet?" I asked.

"Not yet," Jack replied, "but we've got to have one soon because there's a talent show coming up at the school and we want to play. We also need another guitarist and someone who can sing." Jack said that he and his friends were practicing two to three times a week at his drummer friend's house and that they were really "down" for making the extra effort.

Jack's enthusiasm and energy for skateboarding and his music were obvious. I straightforwardly asked Jack how much he cared about school these days. "Not much," he said. "I just want my parents off my back so I can see my friends. Now they are threatening to take my guitar away if my grades don't come up. But I don't know. Are there any pills I can take to help me do better in school?"

Jack is among the many kids his age whom I've been asked to evaluate because they perform poorly in school during what I've come to call their "valley of motivational fatigue" phase. I coined this name based upon a television commercial I remember from the early 1960s for Welch's Grape Juice. A group of students was shown working vigorously at their desks as the clock's hands moved quickly around the dial. Suddenly, at 11 AM, the entire group of children ceased work and slumped over their desks as if hit by nerve gas. The commercial sternly announced that the students were in the "valley of fatigue," caused no doubt by a temporary low blood sugar or something to that effect. Within moments after drinking a glass of grape juice, the children were shown to be revived, once again working industriously.

In naming Jack's problem the valley of motivational fatigue, I wasn't thinking that his slump in effort was merely a quotidian event to be corrected by a jolt of sugar. Rather, Jack had entered a much longer phase of his life, which began around age eleven and would continue until he was about sixteen or seventeen. During this time, his motivation and interest in school would drop into a "valley" and not return until the tenth or eleventh grade, which is about when kids like Jack begin to think of life after high school, and grades start to "count" for college.

Although it has not been formally studied, this drop in motivation and school performance is fairly widespread. I'd estimate that perhaps as many as one in five young male adolescents underperform sufficiently to affect their grades during middle and early high school years, secondary to a drop in motivation and interest in academics. Also during this time, they are no longer as interested in pleasing others and are not as easy to intimidate into performing against their will.

Indeed, although history, math, language arts, and foreign languages may continue to hold the interest of some, these subjects' significance to a majority of students of this age drops significantly. Still, most kids continue to perform well, or at least adequately. These children are likely "pleasers" by nature, young people who developed good habits and grades during elementary school. They continue to enjoy the prestige and social rewards given to them by their parents and school for good performance.

Some of these students are simply bright and can compensate easily to make up for what's nearly a universal loss of interest in the material. However, even for some of these more gifted students, innate intelligence may not be enough in high school or college, when the demands of their classes call for more than minimal effort.

But Jack wasn't that lucky. Never a great student, he had been tested by his school in the past; his IQ was average, but his skills in reading and math were behind those of his peers. Jack operated in the lower quartile of his class, not low enough to qualify for special services or accommodations for the learning disabled, but certainly low enough to make learning or school "not fun." After nine years of formal schooling, it's easy to understand why at this point in his life, Jack might try to avoid work in the classroom and instead socialize with his friends or procrastinate over homework, to the enduring chagrin of his worried parents and concerned teachers.

Jack's problems—his statements that he couldn't concentrate, his teacher's observations of his distractibility and inattention in the classroom, and his parents' inability to motivate Jack sufficiently to perform—should ostensibly meet the criteria for the nonhyperactive form of attention-deficit/ hyperactivity disorder, formally called "ADHD-inattentive type." (Patients, their families, and even professionals increasingly use the simple acronym ADD to describe Jack's problems at school.)

Jack's answers to virtually every standardized questionnaire (which these days have become the main ADHD diagnostic instruments) would result in scores reaching levels of "clinical significance" in the categories of inattention, distractibility, and disorganization. These questionnaires ask only about the behaviors or symptoms of ADHD. They do not investigate the causes of the symptoms, nor are they meant to be used as the sole diagnostic criteria for ADHD. But they have become the sine qua non for the diagnosis of ADHD and the justification for using medication in a kid like Jack.

An "expert" evaluator, such as a general or behavioral pediatrician, a child psychologist, or a child psychiatrist, is supposed to provide the ultimate determination of whether a child has or doesn't have ADHD. But in the absence of any more clear or definitive criteria for the disorder, most doctors, I'm certain, would rubber stamp the results of these questionnaires as "proof" of ADHD in Jack and offer him medications such as Adderall or Concerta. But Jack's symptoms are not caused by ADHD or even ADD in any sense of what the diagnosis used to mean—and continues to mean today if one looks beyond Jack's symptoms.

A few doctors, including me, would be troubled by Jack's obvious lack of motivation toward school, which he so honestly acknowledged in the interview. I would hesitate about using medication right away. I would first try some behavioral and educational interventions, including suggesting to his parents that their responses become more structured and immediate. I'd encourage them to write up a formal, detailed contract for Jack's behavior and performance, with specific consequences and rewards that were meaningful to him. He might benefit from a daily tutor—not one of his parents, but perhaps a college student who could work with him to get his homework done. However, if Jack continued to fail three or four months after a such a program was in place, even I would be willing to offer a stimulant medication if he and his parents were interested.

But I don't believe for an instant that Jack has the kind of disability or problems that were typical of the "classic" ADHD of fifteen years (or more) ago. I've explained elsewhere in this book why I medicate children with stimulant drugs even when I don't believe they really "have" ADHD. But I am troubled by the lack of interest the ADHD academic community has demonstrated in addressing the role of motivation in school performance and in ADHD and its treatment. By "motivation" in this case, I do not mean Jack's response to immediate reinforcers—rewards and punishments—which has been studied extensively in ADHD research. Indeed, persons with ADHD could be defined as having an "aberrant" response to normal reinforcement schedules in comparison with those without ADHD.

My concerns are over the broader role that motivation plays in ADHD diagnosis and treatment for children like Jack who are in a long-term valley of decreased motivation when it comes to school. My confusion led me to reconnect with Russell Barkley, now an emeritus professor at the University of South Carolina in Charleston.[1] Dr. Barkley is known worldwide as a preeminent researcher and theorist of modern ADHD. His articles, books, and public speaking have influenced millions of professionals and patients alike to rethink childhood misbehavior and underperformance in terms of ADHD.

Dr. Barkley and I have run into each other several times, mostly in two-minute "debates" on television. But once, after yet another live panel discussion on ADHD, this one at an American Psychological Association national meeting in San Francisco, I suggested we get together for a drink after the meeting. Russ and I discovered, not too surprisingly, that we agree on more than we reveal on television.

In our most recent conversations, I especially wanted to ask Russ about motivation and ADHD because in the late 1980s and early 1990s, he was theorizing that ADHD boiled down to a "neurological disorder of motivation."[2] He believed that, mediated by innate factors of personality and temperament, ADHD children had different degrees of motivation and therefore responded differently to rewards and punishment than did children without ADHD. Subsequently, for both theoretical and research reasons, Barkley abandoned his motivation theory of ADHD.

In 1996, with the publication of his book *The Nature of Self-Control*, he instead chose to focus on time and impulsivity as the central problems of ADHD.[3] His core definition of ADHD remains applicable today. According to Barkley (whose ideas have been widely adopted by other leaders in the field), ADHD is the relative inability to utilize the knowledge of time-delayed consequences in order to make decisions in the present. To define it with one word, Barkley chose "impulsivity" as the core problem of ADHD.

Ten years later, Barkley remains uncomfortable with the nonimpulsive form of ADHD, ADHD-inattentive type (or informally, ADD), the diagnosis that ultimately would justify giving Jack stimulant medication. "The inattentive type [of ADHD] is a wastebasket diagnosis— beginning with its introduction in the *DSM-III* as a separate category." Russ told me he believes that of those children diagnosed with ADHD-inattentive type, only half have some neurological problem, but even then, it has less to do with attention than with a processing or learning problem. These children have none of the cardinal symptoms of "classic" ADHD—inattention, impulsivity, and hyperactivity— which is now technically called "ADHD-combined type."

"These kids [ADHD-inattentive] are spacey and daydream," Russ told me. "They just process information very slowly. They have learning disabilities. Personality-wise they are shy, inhibited, reticent, and often anxious. They don't have as good a response to stimulants as do the impulsive ADHD kids." (This is not true in my experience, by the way, of treating these children—their responses may be less dramatic than those of impulsive hyperactive ADHD kids, but no less effective.) Jack and many others like him—lacking any clear neurological deficit but operating in the valley of motivational fatigue—would likely fall into the wastebasket diagnosis of ADHD-inattentive type.

Barkley reviewed his work with me on motivation. Here, he was referring to task-specific motivation, not the general and prolonged "valley," which he later referred to as a developmental phase. "ADHD children have a reduced sensitivity to reward, especially delayed rewards." He again emphasized time as the most important distinguishing factor. "Is this an arousal problem, a problem with the reinforcement system, or some other self-regulation issue?" he still wonders. But bottom line, these kids "are not motivated by typical societal reinforcers like grades."

Russ was also quite ready to acknowledge the larger "life cycle" types of decreased motivation. Well aware of the drop in motivation and interest that occurs in early adolescence, he considered Jack's lack of interest in school as "part of normal development, not a disorder, not genetic." ADHD is considered highly heritable by Barkley and other ADHD experts.

He mentioned another "life cycle" group vulnerable to misdiagnosis with ADHD: women at menopause who think they have ADHD but whose real problem is a decline in working memory. These women prefer a label of ADHD to one of very, very early senile dementia (i.e., Alzheimer's). Adderall or Concerta will help in either case—ADHD or Alzheimer's—at least, in the early stages.

And that's the rub for me. It's what bothers me about all this, and it apparently bothers Barkley as well—a reality that our society is facing with increasing frequency. Whether it's ADHD, Alzheimer's, or the valley of motivational fatigue, stimulant medication improves performance of boring and repetitive tasks for everyone, not just children or adults with ADHD.

Russ said he would be very reluctant to treat Jack immediately with a stimulant medication. He agreed with my plan—first, try to change Jack's environment in the hope that he could be motivated positively with cash rewards and extra privileges and avoid consequences he feared, such as losing his guitar. If there were some learning issues, Barkley also would advise tutoring. But in the end, if those measures failed, Barkley would invoke the ADHD diagnosis to "relieve suffering—as a means to an end" in order to prescribe stimulants to Jack.

As an aside, Russ was also very concerned about the misuse and abuse of prescription stimulants by teens and college students. Saying, "I can't give you much data," he recounted numerous anecdotal reports of parents "who will try anything" to improve their children's high school performance. He also knew of college surveys that reveal that on some campuses, up to one in four students has used prescription stimulants illegally to "power study" or just get high.

Ironically, Russ holds MDs like me primarily responsible for this new wave of doctor-prescribed stimulant abuse. His view strikes me as a rather narrow judgment of who is responsible. Over the past twenty years, Russ, a PhD, and countless other psychologists, educators, and mental health professionals have all relentlessly promoted ADHD as an explanation for underperformance at school and have supported treatment with stimulants. Many of the prescribing doctors don't have or don't take the time to properly evaluate for ADHD, and many are not qualified to do so either. They simply approve the diagnosis with a prescription based upon what national and local experts tell them about their patients' problems.

It appears, then, that Russ would also reluctantly support this watering down of the ADHD diagnosis in order to provide performance-enhancing drugs for unmotivated teens (and for menopausal women?). Take my decision to treat Jack with medication and multiply it by the number of doctors across the country doing the same, and you have hundreds of thousands of patients now taking prescription stimulants who probably don't "have" ADHD in any real sense of the disorder.

There are other consequences to using the ADHD diagnosis in order to justify medication for Jack. The diagnosis is technically categorical, but qualities such as paying attention or acting impulsively are in reality dimensional. There are mild, moderate, and severe cases of ADHD. But the *DSM* diagnostic category for ADHD is black or white. Either you have it, or you don't.

Thus, would Jack and his parents—armed with his diagnosis of ADHD—try to obtain accommodations like extra time for test taking at his school or in taking the SAT? I'm certain that cases like Jack's were not meant to meet the stringent criteria set up to qualify for the diagnosis. Yet I know of many neuropsychologists who seem to consistently find sufficient abnormal tests results for kids like Jack to qualify them for accommodations.

However, the ADHD diagnosis, no matter how trivial, could also pose some problems for Jack in the future. Using current ADHD statistics, actuaries are already making health and disability insurance more difficult (that is, more expensive) for those with ADHD. Even in wartime, when the military struggles to fill its enlistment quotas, no branch other than the army accepts those who have been diagnosed with ADHD. In these situations, lumping Jack's life-cycle ADHD in with the problems of other, more severely disabled people could be doing him quite an injustice.

Russ Barkley appropriately cautions that children with "true" ADHD enter the early adolescent years (that valley) with even more risk of performance failure in middle and early high school. The same is true for children with previously existing learning problems. I agree with Russ that these factors are important in school performance. But so is motivation. I've employed an equation of sorts to account for underperformance that includes learning problems, ADHD, and motivation.

The equation is as follows: performance = talent × temperament × motivation. Talent is that range of abilities or skills that are either innate or learned by the child. One can have superior or weak abilities in some or all areas. Extreme weakness in one skill with otherwise normal abilities is categorized as a learning or processing disorder and would fall in under the "talent" category. The tendency to want to please others and the ability to work for delayed gratification are qualities of temperament or personality. So are the qualities of children who are less interested in pleasing others than in following their own interests. The impulsivity of ADHD also is within this category. The ability, or lack of ability, to respond to short-term reinforcement, what is referred to as "motivation" by most ADHD researchers, would actually be included in aspects of temperament.

The motivation factor in my equation of performance refers to much broader fluctuations attached to various phases of the life cycle. So a young adolescent like Jack is more interested in skateboarding and music, both of which take precedence over performing at school, the latter of which is important to other people—his parents—who believe they know what's good for Jack.

There are phases in the life cycle when motivation is likely to increase (without any increase in the immediate rewards or punishments). Jack and most of his underperforming compatriots will become more interested in their school performance as they get closer to the end of high school and realize that grades count for college entrance. This increase, to use Dr. Barkley's language, is also "normative" for the culture.

Finally, the factors in my performance equation are not independent. For example, over time, those who have less talent or who struggle with impulsivity will likely experience a negative impact on their motivation in terms of interest and effort in school-related tasks. A small number of children will not become more motivated. They will give up the chase for "the good college" and settle for a two-year community college, post-high school vocational training, or a job that doesn't require a degree. But even they are likely to try harder as they move into their early twenties. If genetics are as important as Barkley says they are, then I can be confident that most of my ADHD patients will be doing well by their mid-twenties, considering that nearly all the children I see have parents who both work and are in stable relationships.

Regardless of the theory—Russ's, mine, or another's—Jack and thousands like him will be prescribed stimulants. This is the way we handle underperformance because of our culture's obsession with achievement and anxiety over our children's self-image and self-esteem. We may say that Jack's problems at school are the result of his having ADHD, but Russ and I, along with many others in the field, know better. We will continue to prescribe, albeit hypocritically, blurring the boundaries between those with a true lifelong disorder and those only struggling with a phase in their lives. And as we use more and more psychiatric drugs for real or imagined disorders, my ultimate worry is about a society that chooses to cope by using drugs, even those prescribed by well-meaning doctors.

Part III

Drug Companies, Academic Medicine, and the Way We Treat Children's Problems in America Today

11

Strattera, Now Playing Everywhere[*]

The movie *Jaws* broke all previous first-weekend box office receipts when it opened in 1975 and redefined the "blockbuster." Since then, the financial and pharmaceutical industries have designated certain drugs as blockbusters too. Prozac and Viagra immediately come to mind. Given the similarities of the enormous profits and costs of movie and drug development, it's no surprise that the promotional and advertising approaches also are very similar. This brings up Strattera, the new nonstimulant drug by Eli Lilly being pushed for the treatment of attention-deficit/hyperactivity disorder (ADHD).

In the summer of 2004, Lilly offered a press release and followed with letters to physicians that proclaimed, "Strattera Posts Fastest Launch Ever for a New ADHD Medicine with 1 Million Prescriptions in First Six Months." With drug companies already financing educational seminars, "consultant" dinners, free gifts, trips, and charitable donations used to influence doctors' prescribing habits, this particular advertising/psychological approach represented a first for a pharmaceutical product.

---

[*]A version of this chapter was first written in September 2004. It has been updated with more recent information.

Like the movie industry, this drug company is hoping to begin with doctors what economists call "a non-informative information cascade." (I'm indebted to James Surowiecki from the Financial Page of the *New Yorker* for some of these technical terms[1]). People are motivated to see a new movie simply because apparently everybody else is going, so it must be good. In an analogous fashion, doctors and patients are driven to believe this drug must be good, even though there is no data to support its effectiveness and safety outside of industry-supported short-term studies hawked by industry-linked experts and consultants.

Reporting the big opening-weekend box office receipts for movies works only if there's been a massive pre-opening advertising campaign teasing the potential audience with movie trailers, television commercials, and boffo quotes by often-obscure reviewers. Promotion to doctors on Strattera began nearly two years before its release in February 2004, and the scope of the marketing campaign both to doctors and directly to consumers (DTC advertising) in general-interest magazines and television was unprecedented.

Diller in Drug Wonderland

I myself was invited to attend a meeting as a consultant to Eli Lilly. The meeting was to take place over dinner at one of the fanciest restaurants in San Francisco in the Ritz-Carlton hotel. Lilly would also pay me five hundred dollars to "consult." I was intrigued by the proposition. I never accept drug-company money, but I wondered what on earth was to happen at this meeting that would lead Lilly to pay me and at least twenty other doctors that kind of money to attend.

I made arrangements for the money to be sent to the Omega Boys Club of San Francisco, a wonderful organization that supports inner-city African American youth. Then I went to the meeting. The setting was splendid, the meal was reasonable, and the presented information tilted unmistakably toward this "new" nonstimulant that was once considered as an antidepressant. I was unimpressed by the data, and when asked if I would prescribe the medication, I pointed to one of my local pediatric colleagues who is far more adventurous than I in using his patients as guinea pigs for new drugs. I said, "I might try this drug after Stephen has used it for two years on his patients and tells me it's okay." Indeed, after six months, Stephen felt that the drug, to be called Strattera, was quite disappointing and didn't measure up, as I expected, to the stimulants like Adderall or Concerta.

Lilly, like the movie companies, hoped that the early huge marketing campaign would work, based on a phenomenon the advertising psychologists call "signaling." Early on, you can't tell if the movie or drug is any good, so you look for early signs or signals. That's the idea in reporting the first-weekend box office receipts and the results of the first six months of prescribing the drug. This approach works, though, only until the potential viewer, doctor, or patient has seen the movie or used the drug. Once that happens, the actual experience becomes more important than any advertising.

This marketing approach to movies does work for the film business, at least in guaranteeing a big first-weekend box office take. However, many of 2004's summer blockbuster releases, in particular "The Matrix Reloaded" and "The Hulk," died after the first weekend. Hollywood knows that after the first weekend, non–industry-sponsored reviews and—most importantly—"word of mouth" are what give a movie "legs" to make it a true commercial smash hit.

With pharmaceuticals, it's a little bit different. The time frame is somewhat longer. It takes two to three years before some group independent of the manufacturer (sometimes government-financed, now more commonly financed by a competing manufacturer) publishes a review of the pros and cons of a medicine just released. Earlier than that, however, word-of-mouth information exchanged between patients and doctors reaches the interested investor or clinician.

In the first months after its release, I did some informal polling on Strattera with some psychiatrists and pediatricians not connected financially to Lilly. They offered such unenthusiastic blurbs as "remarkably mixed," "will not be a replacement for stimulants," and "three-quarters of those who tried Strattera have come to stimulants, either because of lack of effectiveness or side effects." The long term future for Strattera based upon these reviews did not appear bright, at least for childhood ADHD, for which stimulants have been a mainstay of treatment for decades.

Certainly industry insiders were aware of the early feedback. Their hopes depended on "creating" a market for adult ADHD—a not-so-impossible job. Few remember that "major depression" was a rare diagnosis in adults until Lilly introduced Prozac for the treatment of depression back in the early 1990s. The rest, as they say, was box office history.

By the way, there are one or two differences between a movie and a drug. A movie is entertainment and discretionary. A drug, at least ostensibly, is for health purposes and necessary (though many of our biggest blockbuster drugs, such as Viagra, clearly are enhancers, not treatments). In addition, our health costs are soaring out of control with the cost of pharmaceuticals rising the fastest. Can we justify ethically and economically diverting precious health care resources based upon clever advertising techniques? Perhaps we should ask Steven Spielberg.

A POSTSCRIPT ON STRATTERA (OCTOBER 2005)

Strattera, though commercially quite successful for its manufacturer, Eli Lilly, has been a clinical disappointment—so much so that despite vigorous lobbying from Lilly, the clinicians have unofficially relegated Strattera to the category of "second-line" medication for ADHD, to be used only after trying the two classes of stimulant drugs (methylphenidate, as in Concerta, and amphetamine, as in Adderall).[2] As predicted in November 2004, results of a head-to-head study comparing Strattera to Concerta for the treatment of ADHD were announced.[3] The study, financed by McNeil, the makers of Concerta, demonstrated that the methylphenidate-based product (Concerta) was more effective with fewer side effects compared to atomoxetine (Strattera).

Though Strattera is not abusable, its use is associated with other adverse effects not commonly experienced with the stimulant drugs, especially stomach pain and diarrhea. Also there are reports of sexual side effects (decreased libido) with Strattera. Toxic liver side effects are rare but have been reported.[4] Finally, in September 2005, the FDA required Lilly to add a black-box warning to Strattera's drug label about increased suicidal thinking and behavior, a warning similar to that which appears on the labels of the SSRI antidepressants.[5]

Although the unprecedented DTC marketing created quite an initial demand for Strattera, the unexpected result of the campaign was to increase overall the awareness of ADHD in adults, to whom much of the promotion was directed. Rates of legal prescription-stimulant use have soared for adults in the last four years, some of the increase attributable indirectly no doubt to the Strattera marketing campaign.[6] Unfortunately, adult prescription-stimulant use historically has been associated with the development of tolerance, addiction, and abuse. Evidence from high school and college campuses suggests that this is already happening. Perhaps in the end, ironically, there *will* be a place for Strattera—if adults really want their "ADHD" treated with a mediocre drug.

12

Galileo's Grandmother: What Happens When Your Life's Work Falls Outside the Demanded Result*

In 1633 Galileo Galilei was found guilty by the Catholic church of promoting the heretical notion that the earth was not the center of the universe. Galileo had been warned several years earlier to refrain from such speculation. Yet he'd seen the moons of Jupiter and the phases of Venus through a telescope. Scientist that he was, he couldn't ignore the evidence he had accumulated, even if that evidence supported Copernicus's heliocentric apostasy.

In the end, though, facing a possible death sentence, he chose to recant his position. He lived the remaining years of his life under virtual house arrest at one of the palaces of his supporters. During those final, difficult years, Galileo wrote often to his daughter, Sister Maria Celeste, whose letters to her father were the basis of the best-selling book by Dava Sobel, *Galileo's Daughter*.[1] But what happens today when a scientist's life's work happens to fall outside the result

---

*A version of this chapter appeared in the *Psychotherapy Networker*, 2005.

demanded by the reigning powers? Ask Nadine Lambert. She could have been Galileo's grandmother.

At first glance, Nadine Lambert doesn't look the part of a radical firebrand, bent on undermining the pharmaceutical industry and sticking it to the power elite of the American child-psychiatry establishment. She moves carefully and deliberately, as befits someone who could be a grandmother several times over. Her cropped gray hair and air of resigned world-weariness belie a fierce determination not to back down from the results of her life's work—a study that tracked four hundred children for over twenty years and that raised disturbing questions about Ritalin. She's been a research psychologist in the department of education at the University of California at Berkeley since 1973, and she now heads the department's school psychology program.

Lambert herself never planned on becoming the *enfant terrible* of the world of attention-deficit/hyperactivity disorder (ADHD) treatment. Her work in the field began quietly and methodically in the 1970s, when she became involved in a larger effort to develop special-education services for school-age children. The original purpose of what became her life's work was a straightforward prevalence study to determine the relative number of handicapped or hyperactive children in San Francisco's East Bay area. From the mid-1970s to 1990, Lambert regularly published scientific articles describing an ambitious research project that anticipated following these children to adulthood.

Then, in 1998 this dignified, middle-aged professor of educational psychology suddenly became the center of an academic firestorm. At the prestigious National Institutes of Health Consensus Conference on ADHD, she announced the results of a study suggesting that use of Ritalin, one of the most routinely prescribed drugs for children in America, might contribute to later drug abuse. Her study of nearly 400 children with ADHD showed that by the time children treated with Ritalin reached their mid-twenties, they had double the rates of cocaine abuse and cigarette smoking as young adults who hadn't taken Ritalin in childhood.[2]

If Lambert had lobbed a grenade into her audience of child-psychiatry researchers, her report couldn't have been more explosive. "Maybe I was just insensitive to the possibilities," says Lambert. "I just wanted to know whether their lives were better or worse. And then you discover these serious outcomes." But for proponents of Ritalin and other psychiatric drugs for children—most of the attendees at the meeting—Lambert's findings had nightmarish implications. What if outraged parents now began to flood their offices, demanding to have their children taken off these medications and given alternative treatment? Perhaps even worse, if Lambert was right about Ritalin's dark potential, it meant that the child-psychiatry establishment was wrong. Seriously wrong. Wrong all along. For the ADHD researchers who'd long put their faith in Ritalin—even bet their careers on it—this was truly scary stuff.

Their fears were well-founded. The media picked up on the story and loudly questioned, as it had several times before, whether Ritalin was being overprescribed for children with ADHD and setting them up for future abuse. "I was never against Ritalin, even in the 1970s," says Lambert. "I was never on a mission." However, she has had reservations about the drug—reservations that are shared by many doctors. She says, "I had the feeling, even as I do now, that Ritalin was being offered as a substitute for more help or special education at school. Why bother tutoring him in reading if Ritalin helps his behavior?" But she maintains, "Our study has always been Ritalin-neutral. I've never said that stimulants aren't efficacious. But when I discovered negative consequences, I was obligated to report them."

Before the 1998 NIH conference, Lambert had a premonition that she "might need a bulletproof vest" after she disclosed her results. She was right. The tight-knit community of child-psychiatry researchers and academics wasn't about to roll over in defeat. Instead, within a year, child psychiatrist Joseph Biederman of Harvard Medical School, one of the country's most influential ADHD researchers and a leading advocate for Ritalin use, announced the findings of a rebuttal study. His new research showed that teens prescribed Ritalin actually had an 85 percent lower rate of substance abuse four years later.[3] The study further claimed that the medicated children were actually "protected" from engaging in later drug abuse.

Two subsequent studies by leading researchers Timothy Wilens, a longtime member of the Biederman team, and Russell Barkley, a professor of psychology at the University of South Carolina in Charleston and the world's leading theorist and arbiter of ADHD, also took aim at the Lambert study. These studies differed in design from Lambert's and, as we'll see, also had numerous limitations.

The study by lead author Timothy Wilens described a meta-analysis of seven older studies on the effects of stimulants on drug abuse.[4] Meta-analyses are "in" these days in the world of medical publishing as a way to generate a sufficient number of patients to justify a significant statistical power between multiple variables. If you had trouble with the previous sentence, you are not alone. Basically, meta-analyses are surveys of previous smaller studies; they attempt to collate the data of the smaller studies in order to make broader conclusions. Most medical doctors themselves are not qualified or interested enough to delve into the statistical arcana or the small print describing the methods of a particular meta-analysis. And anyone reading such a study must have a wide breadth of knowledge of the field to know for certain whether all the appropriate past trials were included in the survey—or if poorly conducted trials were excluded.[5] In his meta-analysis, Wilens backs up the claim made earlier by Biederman's team: stimulants, Wilens concludes, are *unquestionably protective* against later drug abuse. In fact, the children in his study who took stimulants were 50 percent less likely to abuse drugs in later years.

In his study, Barkley returned to one of his earliest groups of patients who were first examined in 1979 and then reexamined thirteen years later for substance abuse.[6] His research of 147 children, reevaluated as young adults, found neither a sensitizing nor a protective effect from earlier Ritalin administration. A close inspection of Barkley's own data reveals a pattern of higher rates of substance abuse in the Ritalin-treated group, similar to the pattern found in the Lambert study. For example, in Barkley's Ritalin-treated group of ADHD kids, five of a hundred examined as teens abused cocaine whereas no one in the unmedicated group subsequently used cocaine—a disturbing trend but not statistically significant according to the study. Barkley's conclusions, based on his analysis of the data, appeared to back up neither Lambert's findings nor those of the Biederman group. But in the discussion section of his paper, Barkley uses 267 lines of text to savage the Lambert study—but only twenty-four lines question the conclusions of Biederman and Wilens.

After scaring the public with Lambert's information, the media obligingly switched course upon the simultaneous publication of the Wilens and Barkley studies in the January 2003 issue of *Pediatrics*, now extensively touting the "protective benefits" of Ritalin. The pharmaceutical companies that manufacture Ritalin and similar stimulants reprinted the Biederman and Wilens papers and sent them to every pediatrician and child psychiatrist in the country.

Since this imbroglio, the National Institute of Drug Abuse (NIDA) has refused funding to Nadine Lambert, either to conduct further follow-up on her subjects or to more closely analyze her current data. Recently, a government official privately told her that her latest grant proposals have been harshly criticized during the peer-review process. Since the publication of her original study results, no major U.S. journal has been willing to publish either her new research or a fresh analysis of old research to rebut her critics. She's been dismissed in print by at least one prominent critic as an "outlier on the far end of a bell-shaped curve"—polite academese for a loose cannon whose research is so fringy and unsubstantial that it can safely be ignored. But is it more appropriate to see her as the canary in the coal mine, sounding a warning about the unacknowledged dangers of one of the most widely prescribed drugs for children in America?

DO ALL CHILDREN HAVE ADHD?

No one knows precisely how many children in the United States have ADHD. As with all psychiatric conditions, there's no definitive test for ADHD—no blood test or brain scan or even standardized psychological assessment that can unequivocally determine whether a particular child is or isn't affected. Much of the controversy roiling around ADHD stems from the problem of diagnosis. In its milder forms, the disorder's symptoms of inattention, distractibility, impulsivity, and hyperactivity can look very much like the normal behavior of an active child.

Whatever the problems in diagnosis, Ritalin, along with newer sibling stimulants, have become the overwhelming treatment of choice for children who are "diagnosed" with ADHD. Currently, nearly one in ten eleven-year-old American boys takes some kind of stimulant medication, a classification that included Dexedrine or amphetamine and now includes drugs like Ritalin, Adderall, and Concerta.[7] All told, the United States uses 80 percent of the world's stimulants.[8] Critics of this trend point out that no other country addresses the behavior and school performance of children with such strong emphasis on psychiatric diagnosis and drug treatment.

But why *not* use these stimulants, when they seem to work wonders? This is the standard response of Ritalin's champions, who include legions of grateful parents and teachers across the country. Often, within minutes of taking the first dose, hyperactive Johnny metamorphoses into a different child—steady, focused, and compliant. Skills such as handwriting and following directions improve instantly. Indeed, thousands of studies, mostly of school-age boys, prove the effectiveness of stimulants in helping children perform better at school and at home.

Ever since the first published report on children's use of stimulants in 1937,[9] medical pundits have argued that drugs such as Ritalin operate differently in the brains of hyperactive kids than in the brains of normal kids—because the ADHD brain is different. What else could explain how a stimulant could actually calm a child rather than rev him up even more? It's easy to understand why the assertion that Ritalin calms only hyperactive kids carries so much weight in popular discourse.

But this claim is a myth. In fact, Ritalin and other stimulants improve *anybody's* ability to focus and pay attention to boring and difficult tasks. Studies from the National Institute of Mental Health in the 1970s proved that low-dose stimulants have the same effect on all children (and adults as well), whether or not they've been diagnosed with ADHD.[10] The hyperactive child who slows down on Ritalin appears calmer to parents and teachers, demonstrating that the Ritalin is working. Because the drug works so well, they conclude that the child must have ADHD. But given Ritalin's universal effects on all children, by this logic it would follow that all children have ADHD!

UNDERSTANDING RITALIN'S EFFECTS

Ritalin may help everyone focus, but does it truly calm everyone? In fact, the "calming" effect of the drug on hyperactive kids is actually the result of their becoming more methodical in their performance, which, in turn, moderates their activity level. Indeed, normally active children also become less active when they're given the same low doses of stimulants that ADHD kids get, though the activity slow-down in non-ADHD kids is less dramatic. Similarly, when ADHD children take higher doses of stimulant medications, they react just like other children: both groups become overactive and agitated. Both non-ADHD kids and ADHD kids complain that they feel "nervous" or "weird" on higher doses of stimulants.

Still, Ritalin undeniably helps hyperactive children. Surely, this pharmaceutical leg-up gives these youngsters a much better chance at achieving success as they grow into adolescence and adulthood. But here's the rub: after nearly seven decades of prescribing Ritalin, Adderall, and similar stimulants for millions of children, we still don't know whether these drugs boost kids' chances for success later in life. Given the critical importance of this issue, why are we still so steeped in ignorance?

Part of the reason lies in the daunting challenge of systematically tracking many children for a decade or more. In addition, since stimulants were introduced as a treatment for hyperactivity nearly seventy years ago, diagnostic categories for hyperactivity have changed dramatically. So it isn't clear that earlier studies of the impact of stimulants on hyperactivity examined the same population that today's researchers would be observing. Furthermore, studies done in the 1960s and 1970s were "naturalistic"—the children were separated into treated and control groups based upon their families' choice of treatments—and not randomized, so they're vulnerable to being challenged by today's more stringent criteria.

Finally, whereas virtually all children taking stimulants in the 1970s and 1980s stopped taking them at around age thirteen, when hyperactivity tends to fade on its own, current standards of care mandate that many adolescents continue to take these meds through high school and even into college. Indeed, the only new long-term prospective randomized study in the United States lasted just four-teen months[11] because doctors felt ethically bound not to deny ADHD children access to stimulants required by the American standard of care. So the disappointing outcomes of earlier studies are easily dismissed by medication proponents, who maintain that outmoded definitions of ADHD, changing standards of care, and lack of randomization render the older studies useless.

Still, a handful of ADHD treatment studies were published in the late 1980s and early 1990s, tracking children prospectively from school age into young adulthood. Significantly, these studies also showed disappointing results for Ritalin. Children treated with stimulants did no better (in fact, they did slightly worse) than ADHD kids who hadn't taken Ritalin. In this older research, all three groups of ADHD kids studied—those getting only medication, those getting only family counseling and special education, and those getting a combined treatment of drug and nondrug interventions—did far worse than normal kids, as gauged by rates of high school graduation, delinquency, and drug use. The most rigorous study, done by psychiatrist James Satterfield and his wife, social worker Breena Satterfield, concluded at ten- and fifteen-year follow-ups that the medication-only children did the poorest, and the combined-treatment group did the best.[12]

This isn't to say that stimulants do no good whatsoever. Based on my twenty-seven years of practice, I personally suspect that stimulants can help a kid get through the most difficult years when he's in mandatory schooling. But I believe that long-term outcomes are far more affected by learning problems and emotional problems that have roots in family and community factors.

Researchers and practitioners alike have long been concerned that Ritalin use in childhood could lead to later drug abuse. Lambert didn't invent this issue to annoy the psychiatric cognoscenti or frighten the general public. Ritalin is a potentially powerful addicting agent, classified by the U.S. Drug Enforcement Administration as a Schedule II drug, the strictest category of potentially abusable drugs that doctors are legally allowed to prescribe. Ritalin is a stimulant similar in molecular structure to "speed" (amphetamine), "crank" (methamphetamine), and crack cocaine—all drugs with devastating addictive potential. Laboratory animals, when given the choice of pressing a lever that sends a pellet of food into the cage or one that delivers a methylphenidate (e.g., Ritalin and Concerta) or amphetamine (e.g., Adderall and Dexedrine), quickly learn to choose the drug lever, ultimately starving to death and exhibiting bizarre behavior along the way.

Those animals who are given a dose of amphetamine two weeks or so before an addiction trial begins (a long time in the life of a rat) addict much more quickly and firmly to the amphetamine in comparison with rats who are virgin to the drug at the beginning of the trial.[13] This phenomenon is called "sensitization." Of the neurotransmitters in the brain, dopamine is the one most affected by amphetamine. Apparently, dopamine receptor sites in the rats' brains change even after only one dose of amphetamine. The theory goes that the rat "recognizes" the amphetamine rush when it's been preexposed. The pace of addiction quickens.

Critics of these studies say that giving animals intravenous amphetamine hardly resembles the experience of taking one of the newer, long-acting stimulant drugs such as Concerta. The experience of euphoria, they claim, is based on the *rate* of absorption of the drug into the brain—the faster, the higher. Studies of radioactively labeled drugs in animals show, not unexpectedly, that oral drug ingestion leads to much slower rates of absorption in comparison with abusive methods—hence no high when the drugs are used properly and no higher chance of addiction.[14]

However, studies in normal adult volunteers taking even just one oral dose of Ritalin show very early signs of addiction when the volunteers are given a second dose of the drug several weeks later. Measures of eye-blink and heart rates—subtle markers of addiction—rise in adult humans who take the second dose of medication.[15] As disturbing as these studies are, they haven't generated similar research on kids who take stimulants. No one had quite so clearly and bluntly linked this basic science of stimulant addiction to the real world of hyperactive kids and teens until Lambert announced her findings at the 1998 NIH Consensus Conference on ADHD.

Why, then, has Lambert's study been so roundly dismissed? Her critics contend that her work is simply not up to snuff scientifically, pointing to her study's lack of randomization and the questionable validity of her control groups. Even though her naturalistic approach was "state of the art" at that time, there's no question that Lambert's study subjects weren't randomized into drug and nondrug treatment groups. Thus, despite her prodigious efforts to document the similarities between the two groups, it's quite possible that the sicker and more severely affected kids received Ritalin, and children with milder ADHD didn't. If so, it's logical to conclude that the kids who received the drug might have gone on to have drug-abuse and other problems later in life simply because they were more troubled to begin with.

This well-known study effect, called the "severity bias," could have tilted the scales toward negative outcomes for the drug-treated group. This failure to randomize has also plagued other older studies showing poorer outcomes for young people who took Ritalin as kids. In response to this criticism, Lambert notes, "We were taking a natural sample in the population. Our initial goal was an attempt to determine the prevalence of ADHD in the community. We made a careful effort to find a normal case control for every ADHD kid located."

Lambert's findings have also been criticized for failing to take into account another childhood problem—conduct disorder. This disorder involves a pattern of delinquent behavior such as stealing, cheating, vandalism, physical violence, truancy, trouble with the law, and cruelty to animals. In his published critique in *Pediatrics*,[16] Russell Barkley suggests that the kids who took Ritalin in Lambert's study and showed higher levels of substance abuse later on actually suffered from conduct disorder in addition to hyperactivity. In other words, the medicated kids abused drugs later on not because the Ritalin had sensitized them to other drugs, but because their conduct disorder (which made it more likely that Ritalin would be prescribed for them in the first place) made them more susceptible to substance abuse. Lambert retorts that Barkley's reasoning is circular in that kids who abuse drugs invariably also have conduct disorder, regardless of what originally contributed to their drug use.

Although Lambert's study is certainly imperfect, what's been ignored in most discussions of her work is that the studies cited as rebuttals to her conclusions are susceptible to the same kinds of criticisms. Both Biederman's study and Wilens's meta-analysis were retrospective investigations that were also marred by lack of randomization and by inadequate controls. Moreover, Biederman's conclusions were based on subjects still in their teens who were still taking medication, whereas Lambert tracked her subjects' drug use all the way into their mid-twenties. Even Barkley's study wasn't randomized.

In fact, a dirty little secret of psychology research is that most studies are plagued with methodological difficulties because it's still notoriously difficult to institute unimpeachable controls. "The field is a quagmire," observes longtime ADHD research psychologist Stephen Hinshaw, also of the University of California at Berkeley. "No study can be absolutely free of the possibility of bias or some other unknown variable in the assignment of controls." This is the case for Lambert's efforts, obviously. But according to Hinshaw, it is even more true for retrospective studies. And the Biederman teen study and the Wilens meta-analysis study were both retrospective—that is, they attempted to disprove Lambert by looking back at previous work.

William Carey is the preeminent expert on children's temperament research in America. A pediatrician at the Children's Hospital of Philadelphia, he supports the use of Ritalin but feels that it and the ADHD diagnosis are overused. On the studies of Biederman and Wilens, he is skeptical: "It's more like a religious belief with those guys. You believe in what you want to. They just push the data to have it come out to what they want."

So if the studies that are intended to put the definitive kibosh on Lambert's work are similarly flawed, why can't she get the support she needs to conduct further research on the issues raised? After all, her research was considered vital enough to be funded for twenty years by the NIDA and the California Tobacco-Related Disease Research Program. In addition, one would think that her conclusions are dramatic and disquieting enough to prompt other researchers to reexamine them, utilizing more careful controls and randomization procedures. Why is this unlikely to happen, at least in the United States?

The answer, I believe, has much to do with the politics of American psychiatry and the influence of the multibillion-dollar psychopharmacology industry on scientific debates within the field. Joseph Biederman and his colleagues at the Pediatric Psychopharmacology Clinic of the Massachusetts General Hospital, along with Russell Barkley and other psychiatric specialists in ADHD, are at the center of a seismic shift in the direction of American psychiatry. During the last twenty years, the field has largely reversed course in its thinking about children's behavioral problems, from assigning causation to the child's family and environment to assigning causation to the child's presumably malfunctioning brain. Certainly, once ADHD children begin taking stimulants, the immediate and often global improvement in their behavior reinforces this brain-based line of reasoning—despite the fact that this line of reasoning is seriously logically flawed. Aspirin improves a headache, but no one says that a headache is caused by an "aspirin-deficiency."

This erroneous belief in biological causality is hugely profitable for the pharmaceutical industry, which now earns more than a billion dollars a year from sales of Ritalin, Adderall, and other ADHD drugs. The runaway popularity of stimulants depends, in turn, upon the benediction they receive from leading academic experts, who receive major research funding from more than a half dozen of the world's largest pharmaceutical companies. These days, virtually all leading psychiatry researchers are biologically-oriented scientists who accept funding from pharmaceutical companies. Indeed, drug companies now supply 60 percent of all funding for biomedical research, and that percentage is undoubtedly much higher in the field of psychiatry.[17]

Still, many doctors, both in and out of academic medicine, are troubled by the depth of the clinical research–drug industry connection. In 2000, Marcia Angell, then editor of the New England Journal of Medicine, wrote a stinging editorial entitled "Is Academic Medicine for Sale?"[18] Charging that academic medical institutions are "growing increasingly beholden to industry," she pointed to the potentially corrupting ties binding medical research institutions to drug companies. "There is now considerable evidence that researchers with ties to drug companies are indeed more likely to report results that are favorable to the products of those companies than researchers without such ties," she wrote. "When the boundaries between industry and academic medicine become as blurred as they now are, the business goals of industry influence the mission of the medical schools in multiple ways."

Despite his vigorous stance against Lambert for not predicting that antidrug groups would take up her research as a rallying cry, Barkley treats his Harvard colleagues much more gently when it comes to a similar question of ethics. Ritalin's exoneration by the *Pediatrics* journal articles was extensively covered in the press and on TV. Within weeks, doctors received mailings from the makers of Concerta and Adderall, alerting them about the Wilens article and its conclusions. Not surprisingly, doctors' attention was not directed to Barkley's much more qualified findings in the same journal. Of the pharmaceutical industry's promotional use of the Harvard group's research, Barkley says, "Obviously, they [the drug companies] are involved in their research. I'm not going to defend what the drug companies do. I don't know how much they [the Harvard group] try to stop it."

Others in the field are more critical. "It's appalling," says William Pelham, psychologist at the State University of New York (SUNY), Buffalo, arguably the leading researcher on behavioral interventions for ADHD but also a supporter of the use of Ritalin. "What else do you expect? Biederman and Wilens believe in their results. It's terrible. It's what they do, these companies. Ultimately they are using very poor judgment."

A final word comes from someone who strongly believes in Ritalin for ADHD but still has major doubts about the sensitizing or protective aspects of the drug when it comes to later abuse. Laurence Greenhill is a child psychiatrist and researcher at Columbia University and the author of the definitive text on Ritalin, called *Ritalin, Theory and Action*, now in its second edition.[19] "There's a lot of poetry and metaphor in this area [about Ritalin's later effects]. It's not clear that there's any data regarding sensitization that's been randomized. But I'm not that much happier about the protective side either. Those claims are exaggerated."

FROM NEIGHBORHOOD TO NEURON

Lamentably, we may never learn for certain whether Ritalin contributes to, or protects against, later drug abuse—at least not in any study from the United States. Ritalin, Adderall, and similar drugs have become such accepted treatments for ADHD that it's now considered unethical to withhold them in any randomized, double-blind trial. "Treatment with stimulants has become the standard of care in this country," says University of California at Berkeley psychologist Hinshaw. "Running a study that withheld stimulants for a long time—the ten or fifteen years needed to check for later drug abuse—would be medically unethical in the United States."

But in Western Europe, where doctors don't assign an ADHD diagnosis to as wide a swath of behaviors as do American physicians and where doctors are less apt to use stimulants to treat the disorder, there may still be opportunities to study the question. "The Germans are doing such a study right now," says Hinshaw, "but it'll take years, or we may never know."

American psychiatry and the pharmaceutical industry don't seem particularly concerned about the role of social factors in ADHD and drug abuse (dysfunctional families, bad neighborhoods, poverty, and racism). Millions of American children continue to take Ritalin, Concerta, Adderall, and a host of other stimulant drugs. On another front, the Eli Lilly company, hoping to capitalize on the continuing fears about doctors prescribing drugs with abuse potential, has introduced with great fanfare a drug called Strattera, which is a nonstimulant treatment for ADHD. The drug's major attraction is that, as a nonstimulant, it is theoretically free of risk of abuse. Lilly's strategy to promote this virtue of Strattera may not be far off the mark.

Since World War II, there have been three waves of legal stimulant-abuse epidemics in this country, the last being Dexedrine (the diet pill) in the late 1970s. In each of these waves, the stimulants were first prescribed "legitimately" for an accepted use. Over time, though, the drugs found their way into the abusing population. Often, doctors who were too free in their prescribing of the stimulants became unwitting (or not-so-unwitting) accomplices to patient drug abuse. The lay public and many doctors remain uneasy about the risk of stimulant abuse, despite the efforts of mainstream psychiatry and the drug industry to allay those fears.

There is some irony in prescribing legal stimulants to ADHD teens and adults in order to "protect" them from potential abuse. The question of sensitization to illegal drugs aside, doctors who prescribe stimulants may actually be increasing the chances that America will experience a fourth wave of *legal* stimulant abuse. Already, prescription stimulants such as Adderall and Ritalin are freely traded and sold at high schools and colleges, usually for getting high or "power studying," especially around exam time. Most people can handle an occasional snort of Ritalin without developing an addiction. But the history of stimulant use in America repeatedly shows that a core group of individuals will have trouble controlling their use of the drug and go on to abuse the pharmaceutical product or methamphetamine, its street equivalent.

The truth is that we don't yet know whether Ritalin use makes kids more likely to abuse drugs later on, whether it protects them from later substance abuse, or whether it does neither. What we have are two sets of data, both significantly flawed. One set is accorded great weight and significance by the scientific powers-that-be, and the other is energetically trashed. The data in line with the most powerful economic interests and most influential academic voices are extolled as good science—even "truth"—while the other data are consigned to the dust heap of scientific irrelevance.

In the Middle Ages, Galileo suffered the risk of excommunication and *auto-da-fe* if he didn't retract his conclusion that the earth revolved around the sun. In modern-day America, your "peers" have your journal submissions rejected and your government funding cut off. On the other hand, if your work meets with the approval of the psychiatric–industrial complex made up of doctors and the multinational drug companies, you are hailed as a genius and treated like a prince.

Meanwhile, Lambert, who has now spent nearly thirty years of her life following and analyzing her group of ADHD kids, tries to stay focused and productive. She continues to seek funding for her work, but from philanthropic organizations rather than institutional medicine. She also continues to teach at Berkeley and to write rebuttals to the criticisms of her work, hoping to find a larger forum. "I'm just trying to get answers—it's what keeps me going," she says. But without funds to pursue her long-term ADHD project, she doubts that she can continue the work. "I'm now aiming for a foreign journal like the *Canadian Journal of Psychiatry*," she says. "I doubt that I can get a fair review in this country."

"Maybe I've wasted my life," she says, letting down her professional guard for a moment. She says that she just wants a chance to directly defend her work against the charges of "bad research." But without funds to further pursue her subjects, analyze her data, or have her results published, it's doubtful that she'll be able to continue her work. Unlike Galileo, Lambert refuses to recant. But like Galileo, she's under this peculiar form of research "house arrest"—allowed to "live" in the scientific world but segregated from her peers, with her ideas kept from the "vulnerable" public. Despite Lambert's commitment to her research, her voice is not likely to be heard in this unequal encounter with the powers of establishment science and the business interests of America.

Even though I think Lambert's study has real merit and should be extended, I personally believe that neither the biologically sensitizing nor the protective potential of Ritalin is as important an influence on future drug abuse as environmental factors. Having prescribed Ritalin for twenty-five years—and having seen its short-term benefits a thousand times—my own experience suggests that a child's family and neighborhood are more important than the use of any medication in predicting whether a child will later abuse drugs. If I believed that Ritalin had a strong sensitizing impact on drug abuse, I'd never have prescribed it to most of the children I've treated with the drug.

Ironically, though, the focus on Ritalin as hero or villain suggests just how far the debate has shifted over the years from the influence of the external environment on kids' lives to the internal environment of their individual brain chemistry. Throughout the field, our attention has become increasingly diverted from the roles of family conflict, community breakdown, and poverty as the overriding factors leading to substance abuse in young people. As passions for and against drug interventions grow, they tend to drown out the discussion of nonpharmaceutical interventions for children—family therapy, behavioral interventions, and school-based and community-based programs, for example—that have a proven record of effectiveness in decreasing drug abuse. These days, it isn't just the power and money of Big Pharma setting the agenda. It's also our own professional culture, which seems more and more enthralled by the biochemical fix.

POSTSCRIPT: MAY 6, 2006

Today, when I sat down to read the morning paper, I was stunned to learn about the tragic sudden death of Nadine Lambert. The *San Francisco Chronicle* reported, "Nadine Lambert, a UC Berkeley professor and pioneer in the field of school psychology, died April 26 when her car was struck by a dump truck near campus. [It had lost its brakes at the top of a steep hill and struck her car at an intersection, I subsequently learned.] She was 79." [20] I last spoke to Nadine about two months before her death. She told me that she had had an article accepted by the journal *Addiction*, and was hoping that she would get yet more opportunities to further analyze her data in the process of defending her basic conclusions on Ritalin. She never got a chance to finish her work.

13

Fallout from Pharma Scandals: The Loss of Doctors' Credibility*

In 2004 I attended both Food and Drug Administration hearings on children's depression and antidepressants.[1] Despite my twenty-seven years of clinical practice in behavioral/developmental pediatrics, I was unprepared for the impact these meetings had on me. Listening to the testimony of families whose children had committed suicide while taking one of the new antidepressants—the selective serotonin reuptake inhibitors—left the doctors at the hearing shaking their heads, and watching the intricate dance between government, academia, and industry confirmed my worst fears about the relationship between doctors and the drug industry.

The meetings were the culmination of a decade-long pursuit of justice. In the 1994 case of *Wesbecker v. Eli Lilly*, the family of a man who killed several people and eventually killed himself shortly after starting to take Prozac, sued Eli Lilly.[2] They claimed that Eli Lilly, which manufactures Prozac, knew of its potential side effects and had withheld that information from the public. But when a parade of industry-financed expert witnesses affirmed the safety of the drug, a jury voted nine to three to acquit Eli Lilly. In actuality, Lilly, unbeknownst even to

---

*A version of this chapter appeared in the *Hastings Center Report*, May–June 2005.

the judge, had come to a secret agreement with the plaintiffs' lawyer to settle the case. The presiding judge at one point rejected the jury's verdict. However, on appeal, the case was dismissed. In any case the trial essentially closed the door to successful legal challenges to Prozac for nearly ten years.

Several trial lawyers, convinced of the potential agitating effects of the SSRIs (which, besides Prozac, include Zoloft, Paxil, Celexa, Lexapro, and Effexor), continued to pursue the issue. They were joined in the mid 1990s by a British research psychiatrist and psychopharmacologist, David Healy, whose analysis of studies funded by the drug companies demonstrated a consistent signal of increased suicidality—that is, suicidal thinking and behavior.[3] Their persistent efforts were rewarded when, under the Freedom of Information Act, they discovered eight previously undisclosed studies on the SSRIs and childhood depression.

The new studies had all been filed with the FDA under the Best Pharmaceuticals for Children Act of 2002, which reflected a congressional effort to motivate drug companies to study the effects of medications on children.[4] The effort is important because children's metabolism is different and drugs might affect them differently, but because children present a smaller market for new drugs, the pharmaceutical industry might not study them without some financial prodding. The act rewards the companies that perform pediatric studies by permitting them an extra six months of patent protection, which for a drug like Zoloft represents an additional billion dollars in sales.

However, the law did not require either the companies or the FDA to publicize or publish the findings. In the case of the SSRIs, there were seven existing published studies, of which only three showed that the SSRIs had any benefits over placebo in the treatment of pediatric depression. Healy and company found that all of the eight unpublished studies were negative. When combined with the available public data, the overall numbers clearly showed a lack of effectiveness for the SSRIs and a small but significant increase in rates of suicidality.

The results were first presented to the United Kingdom's FDA equivalent, the Medicines and Health Care Regulatory Agency (MHRA). In December 2003, the MHRA banned the use of most SSRIs for the treatment of childhood depression.[5] The lone exception was Prozac, which had been the subject of the three positive studies.

In contrast, there was evidence of much foot-dragging at the FDA, which operates in a very different "drug culture." In America, beginning in the early 1990s with stimulant drugs like Ritalin, the pediatric use of all types of psychiatric drugs has skyrocketed. For both ideological and economic reasons, the practices of American child psychiatrists changed dramatically over the decade, so that by 2002, nine out of ten children treated by a child psychiatrist were taking one or more psychiatric drugs.[6] In comparison, European child psychiatrists, pediatricians, and family practitioners (who have an important role in child health care in the United Kingdom) are far more parsimonious than their American colleagues with the pediatric use of psychiatric medications.

It was not then until February 2004 that the first FDA meeting convened. By that time, a mid-level FDA official had analyzed the combined data and reached the same conclusion as the British, but his testimony was withheld on procedural grounds that the first meeting's official purpose was only to set up the guidelines for reanalyzing both the public and heretofore secret data. Nonetheless, the public learned of the eight unpublished studies at the February meeting. Drug company representatives meekly explained that they were under no legal requirement to publicize the negative studies, which would have been "contrary to the fiduciary interests" of their stockholders. Similarly, there was no legal obligation for the FDA to publicize the studies. The FDA simply kept them "on file" to meet the requirements of the Best Pharmaceuticals for Children Act.

The discovery caused astonishment, dismay, and anger among those attending the hearing, including doctors, press, and families of suicide victims who had been taking the medications. Here was a case in which the market system, under the current regulatory guidelines, had clearly failed. Profits trumped children's health.[7]

At the second FDA meeting, held in September 2004, the emotions overflowed. "The blood of my child's death is on your hands," seethed a mother of a suicide victim to the FDA psychiatrists sitting on the expert advisory panel. Heeding the pleas of organized American psychiatry, the panel stopped short of recommending an outright ban of use of SSRIs for pediatric depression, but they recommended that the strongest warning, a black box, be added to the labels of all SSRIs. As the panel certainly knew, requiring a black-box warning would effectively end direct-to-consumer advertising for these drugs on television and in magazines.[8]

The meetings had a profound effect on me. My experience with the drug companies, beginning with the marketing of Adderall in the mid-1990s for the treatment of attention-deficit/hyperactivity disorder (ADHD), had already made me skeptical of their claims and cynical about their growing connection to medical leaders in research and organized medicine. Academic medicine, it seemed to me, was being corrupted by its ballooning dependency on drug-company funding.

Leading researchers from the most prestigious medical universities, even as they acknowledged drug-company money for their research and "unrestricted" grants for their speaking engagements, heralded their just-published journal articles on a drug with Wall Street industry–sponsored press conferences. Continuing medical education (CME) has become a means to get around the rules prohibiting advertising for the off-label use of drugs. It gives experts a forum to promote the off-label use of a drug based on "professional experience." As a front-line doctor having to make daily decisions about whom to medicate and not to medicate, I lost faith in my academic colleagues to give me unbiased advice. Real opportunities for cooperation between science, health, and industry have been hijacked by the pursuit of profit.

But now my cynicism about the pharmaceutical industry and skepticism about the advice I get from academic medicine are also shared by the general public. I daily experience this growing public mistrust. Ever more parents question "the data" I present, ask more about long-term adverse effects (my answer most of the time is "No one knows"), and think much more about nonpharmaceutical alternatives.

My recent experience with the Carwell family is a good example of how the pendulum is swinging negatively about all the pharmaceuticals, even with drugs that have a long track record of safety and effectiveness. The school had been complaining all year about the Carwells' son Jimmy's hyperactivity and impulsivity and the disruption he caused in the private school he attended as a second grader. The parents chose me specifically to evaluate their child on the basis of my well-known position on medicating children and on the personal recommendation from a family with a girl in Jimmy's class who had just received an assessment (an assessment that included a "no medication at this time" decision).

Jimmy turned out to be an extraordinary seven-year-old. He had an IQ of 130. He read at a seventh-grade level. He was also one of the most hyperactive and impulsive children I had met in years. Although I felt that certain parenting strategies and classroom accommodations needed to change, Jimmy was your classic candidate for stimulant medication. I reassured the parents that stimulants had been in use for seventy years and had a strong short-term effectiveness and safety record. "But what about long-term safety?" Jimmy's father asked. "And how many of those studies come from the drug industry?" his mother chimed in.

Although I was used to the first question, the second question took me by surprise. In retrospect I should have expected it in light of all the recent publicity on children's antidepressants and the Cox-2 inhibitors (Vioxx, Bextra, and Celebrex). I suspect the Carwells would have been uneasy with psychiatric medication for Jimmy no matter what, but with the recent revelations, their skepticism and anxiety had added power. I told them I understood their concerns and no decision had to be made that day. I said I would try to help them with Jimmy at school regardless of whether they decided to use medication. I gave them some material I had written on stimulant medication and asked them to come back in two weeks to further discuss Jimmy's management. Jimmy's parents eventually decided to give their son a long-acting stimulant that was very helpful for Jimmy at school. But I wondered later on how many families are even more reluctant than the Carwells to consider medication for ADHD and don't even make it to the doctors' office.

THE BLACK BOX: ADVICE TO PARENTS ON THE SSRIs FOR CHILDREN AND TEENS

The FDA now requires the manufacturers of antidepressant drugs to include a black-box warning about the risks of suicide. This is important information for physicians and patients but is bound to cause a lot of confusion and worry. A pediatric panel strongly recommended that the FDA take this action after reviewing studies on the medications' use in children, studies that demonstrated their lack of effectiveness in childhood depression and a doubling of the rate of suicide on the drug as compared with placebo treatment.

I was at the FDA meetings in February and September of 2004. I'm sure the panel was also as affected as I was by the dramatic tragic testimony of family after family whose children died while taking the drugs. But many psychiatrists are concerned that this group of medications, which they still consider quite effective, will be refused by the parents of a multitude of children who could potentially benefit from the drug. What should a parent believe, and should they allow their child to be medicated?

The first thing parents should know is that psychiatric drug prescription for children's depression is much more art than science. Therefore, knowing the biases of the doctor whose advice you're following is quite important. Most child psychiatrists these days are primarily prescribing medication, so there will be a tilt toward their recommending those kinds of interventions. Virtually all the psychiatric researchers who are quoted in the newspaper or television have studies funded by the drug companies or are paid consultants.

I prescribe psychiatric medication to children on virtually a daily basis, but because I publicly challenge the use and overuse of these drugs with children in our country, I have never accepted drug money. Although it means I fly to professional meetings in coach instead of business class, I can't afford the risk to my credibility by accepting money from the drug companies if I also suggest that medication can be effectively and safely used in children.

The antidepressants—and here I'm referring primarily to Prozac and her sisters, the SSRIs, which include Zoloft, Paxil, Celexa, Lexapro, and Luvox—have never impressed me as being particularly effective in treating childhood depression, compared, for example, with the effects Ritalin has on ADHD. This is borne out by the drug-company studies reviewed at the FDA meeting. The studies included 4,600 kids, and only three of fifteen showed the active drug (it was Prozac) as more effective than the placebo.

But not so fast. It isn't easy demonstrating a positive effect on childhood depression because the improvement from the placebo is around 60 to 70 percent in most studies. Any drug would have to be superior to that already-high rate in order to prove its effectiveness. Just last week, this point came back to me in my own practice. A twelve-year-old girl was remarkably improved two weeks after I prescribed her Prozac for what appeared to be a depression with hallucinations (she was hearing voices). She attributed her better mood and elimination of the voices to her taking the medication. I was very impressed. But then later her parents called to remind me that they had decided to give her a vitamin pill instead of the medication because they were nervous about the Prozac; I'd forgotten. One more cure by placebo.

So even if a psychiatrist is convinced that antidepressants work, the science for the moment doesn't support that position. However, the drug could still be used in children. Evidence for Prozac's effectiveness in treating childhood anxiety is much stronger (but professionals and parents should first consider cognitive behavioral therapy, which works as well as medication in relieving the problems of anxiety in children). Even using an SSRI for depression could still be justified, but expectations should be realistic.

It's worthwhile to remember that this is the *second* class of drugs that had proven effectiveness in the treatment of adult depression but failed to demonstrate effectiveness in the younger-than-eighteen age groups. Prior to the early 1990s, the tricyclic drug class (the best known today are imipramine, or Tofranil, and amitryptiline, or Elavil) was studied in both adults and children for the treatment of depression. Before the SSRIs, the tricyclics too "worked" in adult depression but not for the depression of children.

What is so unique about being under eighteen? Clearly the biology of a sixteen-year-old is not so different from that of a nineteen-year-old.

The difference leading to children's lack of response to these drugs is more sociological than biological. In our country, eighteen marks the legal (not biological) age that children have adult rights and responsibilities. Age eighteen is the year most children socially move out of their homes to colleges. Even if they are not going to school, they are more able to leave their homes successfully, both emotionally and economically, by the time they are eighteen.

This greater independence decreases, I believe, the power of the children's immediate environment to influence their experience and ultimately their neurochemicals and behavior. My theory on why the SSRIs and tricyclics haven't been shown to be effective in children is based on this aspect of what we know about brain physiology—that the environment also affects brain chemistry and function. The chemical environment of the brain certainly determines behavior.

We can alter that brain chemistry only so much with our medications. Most children fail to show major improvement for depression when taking these drugs because the effects of their environment—until about the age of eighteen—are too absolutely powerful on their brain chemistries to be tipped by using pharmaceutical drugs. Ironically, the failure of the SSRIs to demonstrate effectiveness in treating children's depression is strong theoretical evidence for the power of environment on children's lives.

I would still consider using these medications for teenagers who are actively suicidal or have tried to kill themselves recently. Teens who self-mutilate would also be a case serious enough to warrant exploring whether medication could be helpful. These children should be followed closely with visits and phone checkups in the first weeks of treatment and any time there is a increase in the dosage.

Although there are many SSRIs to choose from, Prozac, or the now-available cheaper generic form, fluoxetine, was the only SSRI of the bunch that demonstrated effectiveness in the three of fifteen studies that were positive. It is not at all clear why Prozac "worked" and the other drugs didn't, given that they are all very similar in structure and action. Perhaps Prozac's very long length of action has something to do with the difference. Once stable blood levels are reached, the drug stays in the system for up to two weeks even if the person doesn't take any more. The other medications clear the body within a day and require daily dosing to maintain blood levels of the drug.

The most important take-home message, though, is about the side effects. Prior to the FDA warning, if a child started an antidepressant and complained of feeling worse, anxious, agitated, or extremely restless or reported thinking thoughts never thought before (such as killing himself or his parents), the doctor was likely to reassure the patient and his parents: "Hang in there. It's your depression. The medication takes two to four weeks to work. You'll feel better soon." Sometimes the doctor would increase the dose or even add a second medication.

The message from the FDA is: STOP! If the patient's condition worsens in the first days or weeks of treatment, stop the medication—there is a small group (about 4 percent) of kids who seem worse off on the medication. It may be necessary to hospitalize the child (on no medication) until the drug effects wear off. One could try another medication then but only under very tight supervision, and perhaps treating the child without any medication may be the best course for that child.

If your child is already taking the medication and is doing better, you don't have to stop (though it may only be the placebo effect). However, if you plan to stop the medication, don't do it abruptly. It turns out that despite years of denial from the drug companies and their professional experts, there is a mild to moderate withdrawal from the SSRIs—mostly headache and feeling lousy. It isn't the depression returning as claimed for many years. Just ask the mothers who took an SSRI during pregnancy about their babies. In a study of newborns whose mothers took Paxil, the babies were jittery and ate poorly for two weeks after birth. I don't think anyone believes these babies were depressed.

TREATMENT FOR AN AILING TRUST

To be sure, not all of the uncertainty over psychiatric drug use in children is bad, and much of it is long overdue. The public had been misled by the print ads and commercials showing the smiling faces of "successful" children taking the medication. But public mistrust of the drug companies will inevitably extend to distrust of physicians themselves. And why shouldn't it, in light of industry funding for national conferences and their product "bazaars," the continual onslaught of drug detail men with their insidious offers of "free" samples of high-priced brand-name medications (often no better than the cheaper generics), and offers of free dinners with five hundred dollar "consultant" fees that make me feel like a prostitute. American medicine risks returning, ironically, to the era of "patent medicine," when hucksterism and medical practice were synonymous.

Unless clear boundaries (legal and economic) are drawn between profit-driven companies and people's health, doctors will lose their aura of scientific objectivity, so hard-won in the first half of the twentieth century.[9] First, medicine's financial links to the pharmaceutical industry must be limited. The funding of medical education must come from elsewhere, either from the government or out of doctors' own pockets. Industry support of national professional organizations must end. The practice of drumming up business with free samples must end. And new regulations must be enacted that, while allowing for some industry support of research, absolutely protect and guarantee scientific interests. New rules for a central public registry of all clinical trials, from inception to completion, have been adopted by the major medical journal editors, but they are likely to be surpassed by more stringent regulations from Congress. I have wondered whether something along the lines of "blind" trusts for medical research could work, if the drug industry was willing.

Finally, direct-to-consumer (DTC) advertising should be curtailed. The drug industry's claims that DTC advertising serves the goal of patient education ring as hypocritical as those claims about doctors' CME.[10] The United States is one of only two countries in the industrialized world to permit this practice.

These reforms are not likely to be enacted. But after listening to the parents' cries at the FDA hearings and then coming home to find that patients' skepticism has filtered down to the daily encounters in my office, I am certain that if we don't mend our ways as a profession, we will dishonor ourselves as doctors and rightfully lose the public's trust. Doctors, heal thyselves.

14

Successfully Marketing Incompetence: The Triumph and Tragedy of the Therapy/Pill Culture

In my twenty-seven years as a behavioral pediatrician, I've asked more than 2,500 children, "Why are you here?" when evaluating them for learning or behavior problems. A majority of kids over six years old (I don't usually ask children younger) answered, "I don't know" most of the time, even when I strongly suspected they knew quite well why their parents had brought them to see me.

So I was struck when, in May 2005, I asked a nine-year-old boy named Joey this question and he told me, "Because I can't concentrate or focus. I get distracted." His answer was specific and directed, and I was intrigued. He was not alone; increasingly, younger and younger children were offering me a similar response. Mind you, children having problems at school or home had been coming to my office for more than two and a half decades. Why were the children in this new group suddenly defining their problems in this very precise way?

It was fifteen years ago that a parent first asked me, "Do you test for ADD?", and I remember that I had the same reaction. "How odd," I thought. A parent had never before been so direct in asking about a diagnosis. Then (as now), there was no "test" for ADHD, but I understood what she wanted to know. Still, I wondered, where had she gotten the idea to inquire about a test for a specific condition?

Now, looking back, I know. In 1991 the Individuals with Disabilities Education Act (IDEA) was amended to include ADHD as one of the diagnoses that makes a child eligible for special services and accommodations in public school.[1] Once word spread among parents that an ADHD diagnosis opened the door to special help for their children, an "epidemic" of newly diagnosed ADHD spread throughout our country. Now parents "knew" what was ailing their child—or at least they knew the magic words that could make a public school system change the way it dealt with their child.

Doctors, especially psychiatrists, have been changing their view of children's problems since the 1970s. Before then, based on the Freudian model, Johnny's problems were considered the result of inner conflicts generated primarily by his relationship with his mother. But in 1980, with the publication of *DSM-III*, a new concept—for most psychiatric conditions, including ADHD—was announced.[2] These "disorders" were ostensibly based on a collection of symptom behaviors that were assumed to have a biological basis in brain chemistry and heredity. But it really wasn't until 1991 and the change in the IDEA laws that the label took on pragmatic significance.

The diagnosis of ADHD and the use of drugs like Ritalin rose at rates never before seen in this country—or anywhere else, for that matter.[3] The year 1991 marked a veritable sea change—a social movement began that changed the way our society views children's misbehavior and underperformance. Doctors started a public-education campaign directed at parents and teachers, and the latter group began to have an even greater impact on who was seen for an ADHD evaluation. Teachers were instructed to view any underperformance or unruly behavior as a possible symptom of ADHD. In parent–teacher conferences, in notes home, and in school-based evaluations, the message to parents across the country was clear: your child may have a biologically based brain disorder and should be checked by his physician for ADHD (and considered as a candidate for medication too).

The school-led drumbeat for ADHD became so strong that parents began to rebel against the pressure. Several celebrated court cases that related to child protective services' involvement in parents' refusal to medicate their children for school highlighted an anti–ADHD medication backlash.[4] Many states passed laws prohibiting teachers or school psychologists from mentioning ADHD or medication to parents. Finally, in 2004, an amendment to the IDEA reauthorization plainly stated that school districts could not prevent a child from attending school based upon parents' refusal to give psychiatric medication to their child.[5]

However, by then, the pharmaceutical industry had picked up the ADHD diagnosis/medication football and begun running with it. Sometime during the early 1990s, the drug industry hijacked U.S. psychiatry and its new neurobiological identity. Dominating both academic research funding and physician education, the drug companies marketed their products ever more aggressively, at first to doctors and then, in 1997, directly to consumers.[6]

In the late 1990s, in print ads and television commercials, the drug companies began relentlessly promoting the concept of underperformance and certain forms of childhood misbehavior as symptomatic of ADHD. Ads showed pictures of perfect-looking children behaving perfectly. Slogans such as "Reach for the stars" or "Make your child's hidden potential known" were regular components of these slick and not-so-subtle campaigns.

Drug-industry advertising had its effects. First, it propelled Adderall, a not particularly unique amphetamine combination, ahead of Ritalin as the most commonly prescribed trade stimulant drug. Second, it made the acronyms ADD and ADHD common everyday phrases in every U.S. household with children. It was not so surprising then that about four years ago, the first teenagers began asking me directly for a drug to "help them concentrate."

To be sure, there were still teenagers who were highly resistant to taking any medication that might affect their own sense of control or self-image (unless, of course, it was a legal or illegal drug obtained from their friends). But increasingly, struggling, passive teenagers were requesting stimulant medication for school-performance problems. A few were even sophisticated enough to ask for the drug simply for test taking.

Indeed, the effects of stimulant medication on children's behavior in the classroom can be dramatic. I've never been against Ritalin. I've prescribed stimulants to children (and some adults) for a quarter-century. But this new group of teens requesting medication troubled me. I had little doubt that the medication could improve their performance. A few even met my criteria for ADHD. But many seemed very unhappy, alienated from their parents and other adults, and quite unmotivated to do much schoolwork. The request for medication seemed like a further extension of their decision to opt out—to take the easy route—which was, in part, the source of their problems.

They might, in taking the drug, also receive confirmation that there was "something wrong" with their brains. Certainly, in the case of severe ADHD (or for that matter, other physical or developmental problems), neither children nor adults should be held morally or emotionally responsible for tasks they can't do. It would be cruel, for example, to punish someone with a limp because she couldn't run the race as quickly as everyone else. On the other hand, even people in wheelchairs should be held accountable to the level of their competencies. What worried me about these teens was their fixation on the "can't," when I was fairly certain that they *could* if they were happier, more motivated, or better monitored, among other things.

And now the idea of "can't" has reached down to the level of fourth-graders like Joey. No doubt many children with moderate or severe ADHD have been helped by the label and by the understanding that it is hard for them to control their behavior; that, given their personalities/disorder, special ways of handling them—specifically, more immediate rewards and punishments—should be instituted; and that medication can be quite helpful to them and in their management at home and in classrooms.

However, given the bell-shaped distribution of children's ability to concentrate (at either end, a few children focus extremely well or extremely poorly), based on statistics alone, most children labeled ADHD have borderline or mild ADHD symptoms. As for this large group, I'm nowhere as certain that the "can't" concept is helpful or that medication is necessary. As a solution-oriented doctor searching to promote the strengths within those like Joey and his family, I find that each year, as I push my Sisyphean boulder of competence up the hill of our problem-saturated society, the slope of the incline grows increasingly steep.

I used to believe that our infatuation with ADHD and stimulant and performance-enhancing drugs was a product of corporate consumer fundamentalism, a religion of sorts for our culture. Our society's credo, announced every eight minutes in a sermon otherwise known as a television commercial, is "You will be happy if you buy this." No matter the allure of material goods offering spiritual and emotional contentment, however, the pursuit of performance at all costs doesn't explain the growth in the popularity of other psychiatric drugs, such as Prozac, for both children and adults.

To fully understand our heavy use of psychiatric medication, we have to go beyond capitalism and our own shores and understand a cultural phenomenon that has taken hold in most of the Western world. It has been dubbed the "therapy culture" by a British sociologist, Frank Furedi, who posits that as belief in traditional values (exemplified by organized religion and a politics of meaning) has declined, a new, higher valuation on feelings has risen.[7] How we feel, how we feel about ourselves, whether we feel good, and the level of our self-image and self-esteem have become much more important over the last fifty years.

We dwell on our feelings. We believe them to be very important and think we should feel good, at least most of the time. An industry has developed around professionally assessing our feelings and keeping us feeling good. This is the therapy industry, which is part of the therapy culture. The therapy culture has designated "feeling bad"—which heretofore would have been considered a normal variant of human coping—as deviant, pathological, and "disordered," to be treated or cured. The therapy industry and the pharmaceutical companies that have come to dominate it are sincere in their efforts to promote good feelings and mental health. Their track record is another story. Indeed, most measures of mental health and satisfaction seem much more related to achieving a certain standard of living and resolving major economic inequities among the social strata.[8]

So as the gap between rich and poor in this country grows, more people say they feel worse.[9] The therapy industry, meanwhile, continues to broaden the parameters of what constitutes mental illness or disease. Whether it's ADHD, social anxiety disorder, or depression, the television ads tell us we should check with our doctors and seek treatment. The industry (doctors and drug companies) claim they are simply providing a public health education service as they succeed in having more and more unrecognized disease recognized and treated.

Although this may be true to a degree, when I hear nine-year-olds telling me they can't concentrate (and may have ADHD), I worry about the therapy culture that has so completely swept the nations of the West. It is true that, for various reasons, in the United States we medicate our children with psychiatric drugs ten or twenty times more than do the countries of Western Europe. Still, this loss of self-agency and competency, this belief that a doctor or medication is required to solve these allegedly brain-based problems, increases the difficulty of my work with the children and families I treat.

The threat to our country's health goes beyond the challenges I face with Joey in my office. Ironically, as more and more "diseases" are recognized, the boundaries of illness move further and further into the realm of basic human coping. We see it in the broadening of the definition of ADHD, and we see it in the treatment of depression. The relentless increase in health care costs (estimated to be 20 percent of the overall GNP by 2015)[10] is making all our manufactured products, such as cars, more costly and less competitive in world markets. But apart from the drain on our economy, as a nation we will feel sicker and sicker until we move away from the medical model and therapy culture and begin to view most of our major health issues (mental and otherwise) as manifestations of inequitable economic and social factors.[11]

American medicine has never been very good at looking at the broad reasons for ill health, tending to focus on the individual.[12] In this book's first essay, I referred to the comparison between treating ADHD with stimulants and treating diarrhea caused by a factory's pollution upstream. Of course I must treat the individual to relieve her symptoms, but I must also alert others to the conditions creating the individual's illness. Not to do so is to become complicit with forces that may be promoting illness.

I am not alone in my concerns. The World Health Organization, among other institutional groups, has recognized this problem and is beginning to promote models and classification systems based on health and functionality rather than illness and disability.[13] Changing models will be a tough fight here in the United States, where the medical, therapy, and pharmaceutical industries are making major profits from an illness/biology-based model.

Still, regarding little Joey in my office, I'll keep working with him, his family, and his school. I will appreciate his weaknesses, but concentrate on his strengths, his family's strengths, and the positive power of his community in order to improve his life. Outside the office, I'll continue to alert parents, teachers, doctors, and the public at large to the insidious effects of promoting the disease model of behavior and its consequent disempowerment of the Joeys in our community and across our nation.

Professional and Family Factors: A Personal Postscript

I have always been a medical outsider. When I first became profession-ally involved with children's behavior, I didn't intend to become an outsider. My interest in medicine began with my father, who was a family doctor, known in those days as a GP. He had been a specialist in Europe before World War II, but when he arrived in this country with my mother in 1947, he was in a hurry to rebuild a life nearly lost in Europe. So he studied English, took his medical-licensing exam, and decided to eschew the long residency required to regain his specialist status in rheumatology (at that time, a science focused on rheumatoid arthritis). Instead, after finishing a one-year internship, he set up a gen-eral practice in the New York City borough of Queens.

As a child, I experienced my father's medical practice intimately, given that our family lived above his office for the first eleven years of my life. Our house was an old brownstone in a section of Queens that was much like Brooklyn (more city than suburban), with attached homes, kids playing stickball and ring-a-levio on the street until it got dark, and Italian *nonnas* [sic] watching over everyone from stoops and windows. At the end of his workday, my father got down on the floor and played with my sisters and me, quite happy to act silly and clown around with us. I now recognize that my mother's tireless limit-setting and worrying allowed him the luxury of being the "fun" parent. But his playfulness, as a man and respected professional, was, I think, a key influence in my upbringing and thinking and in my eventual decision to become a pediatrician.

My father never pressured me to become a doctor; indeed, as a college student, I was first attracted to the study of law or political science. Over time, however, I realized that, temperamentally, I was drawn to what I felt was the nobility of the practice of medicine. I saw the pleasure and pride my father took in his work. The idea of helping people and earning a good income to boot resonated more deeply with me than the notion of representing people whom I couldn't morally support or wrestling with the ethics of the business world. When I was accepted to the College of Physicians and Surgeons at Columbia University, my father was quite proud. During his internship, he had dreamed of Columbia—then, as now, a highly prestigious medical school—but his background and lack of fluency in English had precluded his admission.

Columbia's influence on me was decidedly mixed. I no doubt received an excellent education at P&S, as we called the College of Physicians and Surgeons, but I gradually developed a sense that the highly trained doctors who were my teachers were more interested in their specialty's organ system than in the overall health and welfare of their patients. I felt alienated by their priorities and style. The pediatricians and pediatric subspecialists were the exceptions.

Perhaps because children cannot be forced to cooperate, pediatricians, even the august specialists, had to literally come down to the level of the child he or she was examining. In particular, I vividly remember a world-famous pediatric neurologist, Sidney Carter, coauthor of *the* textbook on child neurology,[1] getting down on the floor to play with a five-year-old in order to examine him. I loved the way Carter incorporated the neurological exam into his play with the child. How unpretentious and different this man was from many of the other white coats I was following. When I rotated with Carter into adult neurology, I noticed that his adult patients responded equally well to his enthusiasm. Also, the pediatricians seemed the least pretentious of the specialists. Perhaps one reason was that their specialty commanded the least income in comparison with the income of surgeons, ophthalmologists, or dermatologists. Still, money was never a factor in my choice. I thought I could do well enough as a pediatrician (this was 1975—times have changed, even for doctors), and in the end, I felt I could be much more myself in dealing with children.

In 1976, I began a pediatric residency at the University of California, San Francisco (UCSF). I chose San Francisco because I needed a break from New York City, and I also preferred UCSF's informal atmosphere. Everyone called one another by their first names, not all the doctors wore ties, and some even abandoned their white coats entirely. This West Coast style was refreshing compared to the stuffy formality of the East Coast's Ivy League institutions. Later, I came to recognize that these behaviors were only skin-deep, so to speak; as the years passed, I noticed the same cutthroat competition between doctors and departments in California as I had observed at Columbia—academic medicine is tough everywhere, it would appear. At UCSF, they just smiled more.

It was at UCSF, within the division of behavioral/developmental pediatrics—then called the Child Study Unit (CSU)—that I inadvertently discovered my calling. I was unaware of the CSU when I applied for and was accepted to a pediatric residency at UCSF. However, all interns spent a week there, accompanying a child with learning and behavior problems through a gamut of evaluations with a series of experts. That week changed my life.

Here was a group of medical doctors—pediatricians, psychiatrists, and neurologists—along with non-MDs, such as psychologists, speech-language experts, and special education teachers, working together to evaluate and develop a plan to treat children and their families. The notion of including the whole family in the evaluation and treatment plan was revolutionary and greatly appealed to me. Earlier, at Columbia, I had seen how pediatricians were able to skillfully interact with both parent (usually the mother) and child during the course of taking a history, performing a physical exam, and delivering findings. Now, my professional interest in and facility with family systems and family therapy was solidified.

During the mid-1970s, child psychiatry departments in the United States, including those at Columbia and UCSF, were still dominated and controlled by classical Freudian analytical ideas. Indeed, the notion of meeting the child with her parents and siblings was considered heretical (even dangerous) by the Freudians. When Alan Leveton, a UCSF psychiatrist, became interested in family therapy (which started with the work of anthropologist Gregory Bateson in nearby Palo Alto in the late 1950s[2]), he had to relocate his practice to UCSF's pediatric department rather than remain at Langley Porter, the psychiatric facility just across the street.

The pediatricians of the CSU were interested in family. A pioneering pediatrician, George Schade, began the CSU in 1948, and Helen Gofman was his first behavioral pediatrics fellow; in the late 1960s, she took over as the division chair. Helen struck me as an amazing doctor when I met her for the first time in 1976. Her ability to connect and empathize with children, parents, and other professionals astounded me and even today remains an example I try to emulate. Helen was also frustrated and limited by the Freudian model, which posited that children's misbehavior and emotional problems were the results of unconscious unresolved conflicts with their parents, especially their mothers. This conflict, often conceived as sexual by the Freudians, was encapsulated by the "Oedipus complex" (after the Greek myth of Oedipus, who unknowingly kills his father and marries his mother). Decades later, I can see some value in the metaphor, but in the 1970s, adherence to this model of child psychiatry was astonishingly rigid and, ultimately, limiting.

To the pediatricians of the CSU, meeting with only the child in play therapy was too constrictive and pragmatically ineffective for the problems we were treating. True, within the Freudian model, the child's parents could be seen by another doctor, but that struck me as inefficient and less effective than the same doctor treating both parents and child.

From Helen, I also received further reinforcement for my own skepticism about diagnosis in children's mental health. "You're better off describing the child in terms of strengths and weaknesses rather than limiting her to a label," I remember her telling me. The other doctors at the CSU concurred.

After I completed my pediatric residency, the CSU became my professional home for three years of a postdoctoral fellowship. Initially, I thought this would simply help me become a better general pediatrician because I had already realized that, other than the runny noses and the shots, mothers brought children in to see the doctor most often because they were either acting up at home or doing poorly in school. However, while at the CSU, I became aware that some of the behavioral pediatricians had begun private practices as subspecialists in the Bay Area, and I decided to take a chance and do the same.

It was a risky endeavor. In 1980, there were only three behavioral/developmental fellowship programs in the country. Now, there are about sixty, and behavioral/developmental pediatrics is a recognized, board-certified specialty of the American Board of Medical Specialties. But back then, many were confused by my professional practice and identity. (For years, insurance and managed-care companies had trouble classifying me. "Are you a medical doctor or a psychiatrist?" they would ask.)

Local doctors and patients have had no trouble with my background and expertise, however, and they utilize my services extensively. I evaluate and treat families with children who struggle, at home or at school, with behavior or learning problems. During the course of twenty-seven years, I've met with approximately 2,500 families. My longevity in one location has also allowed me to personally follow children I met as six-year-olds into their mid-twenties.

I've never believed that environment (the relationship with parents) was the only thing that determined a child's future. This doubt was confirmed by my experience in the hospital nursery and by research into childhood temperament performed by psychiatrists such as Stella Chess and Alexander Thomas[3] and the pediatrician, T. Berry Brazelton,[4] which demonstrated that children are born with inherent personalities that affect their behavior. I also felt that each child brought an inherent talent profile to their interactions, first with their family and then within their school setting. At the extremes, deficits in language development and visual and auditory processing could express themselves as learning disorders in the school-age child, even those of overall average intelligence. Such variations of personality and intelligence were hardly mentioned by mainstream child psychiatrists prior to 1980.

With the introduction in 1980 of the third edition of the *Diagnostic and Statistical Manual of Mental Disorders (DSM-III)*,[5] American psychiatry shifted its focus away from environmental influences and began to promote a view of child behavior that was solely dependent on the brain, biochemistry, genetics, and drug treatment. On the other hand, the *DSM-III* brought no change to the aspects of childhood mental health and disease that I considered to be important. To my chagrin, even with this shift from environment to brain, the *DSM-III* continued to focus on the individual child rather than the child within the context of family and school and further increased the effort to classify and categorize variations in children's behavior and performance as pathological diseases or disorders.

In some ways, this drive toward classification made sense. The Freudian model allowed for a great deal of wriggle room; never really intended as a scientific model, it operated more as a philosophy (or a theology, according to some of its critics). One of the factors that led to the creation of *DSM-III* was the inability of psychiatrists to agree on what they were seeing as the child's problem. This failure to agree on the definition of symptoms led to a crisis in psychiatry as a scientific field within medicine. If the field's professionals couldn't agree on diagnosis, then how could they effectively conduct research? If psychiatric professionals couldn't conduct research, how could the position that one treatment is effective—or more effective than another—be justified? These questions became crucial to American psychiatry in the 1950s and 1960s, as third-party-payer insurance started becoming almost universal. As the health-insurance business mushroomed, accountability became paramount, not only intellectually and professionally, but economically as well.

It was because I thought its classification system might have some value in research that I initially felt the *DSM-III* was an improvement over the previous version. However, I never saw it as a clinical tool; too many children's problems don't fit neatly into its categories. When the *DSM-III* first appeared, I was not yet aware that organized psychiatry had also developed the manual to promote a biological agenda for children's behavior. The dream was that psychiatry could adopt the medical model, which came out of the nineteenth-century work of pioneers like Koch and Pasteur, who were able to prove that particular bacteria produced specific illnesses. Later, with the advent of vaccines and antibiotics, physicians could actually alter the course of a specific disease and move from handholding into the realm of science.

In many ways, the medical model has served both patients and the profession well. But the utility of the medical model belies its oversimplified and reductionistic aspects. Even Pasteur recognized that sociological aspects could make a person more susceptible to a pathogen (tuberculosis bacillus, for example)—that disease also had to do with living conditions and economic status. This broader interaction between pathogen, the individual, and her environment is best described by the biopsychosocial model first espoused in the 1960s by George Engel, an American medical internist.[6]

The biopsychosocial model applies to all illness, but seems especially suited for psychiatric problems. A person's behavior reflects, in part, a number of inherent factors of biology and genes, manifested as personality and talent (the "bio" of the biopsychosocial). Emotions (the "psyche") are affected by physical health, yet emotional factors also certainly affect how a person feels physically. Finally, experience within the environment (the "social") affects a person's biological processes and emotions. All three factors (bio-psycho-social) reciprocally interact and impinge upon one another.

American psychiatry in the 1960s and 1970s could have chosen to lead the practice of medicine toward the intellectual and ethical position of the biopsychosocial model. But instead, its academic leadership, facing a professional identity and financial crisis, chose to throw its weight behind the medical model, which kept psychiatry within the medical establishment. Ironically, the specialties of family medicine and, to a lesser extent, internal medicine are the groups that maintain the intellectual and pragmatic flame of the biopsychosocial model that the American psychiatric establishment abandoned in its quest for legitimacy.

I am inherently skeptical of the labels and categories we use for children's psychiatric diagnoses. I could invoke my training or numerous erudite scientific treatises on the weaknesses and disadvantages of psychiatric diagnosis in children to explain my position, but perhaps my unease also has something to do with my neither-fish-nor-fowl status within the professional mental health world. However, if I am honest, I must admit that I think my bias began much earlier.

My parents survived the Holocaust. Their losses made me personally aware of the danger of categories and stereotypes. For me, the oldest child of Polish/Jewish immigrant parents, the potential risks of labeling someone as having a biological disorder are not abstractions. Growing up, I heard firsthand the accounts of people who navigated the nightmare of Nazi racial policies. Although some may think it extreme or paranoid to have similar concerns about diagnosis in child psychiatry, they should ask people who were labeled with ADHD or took Ritalin as children if they can obtain medical insurance as young adults, or if they've ever been denied entry to the armed services or another job because of their "history."

I am not against considering the effects of biology and genes on behavior or the use of pharmaceutical drugs for children; nor do I deny, for that matter, the value of occasionally employing psychiatric diagnoses to describe children. But I *am* firmly committed to a biopsychosocial model of children's health and illness. This position anchors the essays I wrote for this book. I write primarily to address the professional moral contradictions and qualms I face every day in my practice of behavioral/developmental pediatrics. I have few illusions that the social conditions that trouble me in my role as a doctor or as a citizen are likely to improve, or even change, in the near future. The trends that disturb me are an integral part of our economic model, our politics, and our culture.

However, although I am pessimistic about our society in the near-term, when it comes to the outcomes for the children and families who come to see me, I am quite optimistic. Indeed, unshackled by a strictly biological and genetic orientation to their problems, I am free to pursue the belief that these children can and will improve with the help of their parents and teachers. Many parents (and children) have told me that they felt this optimism on their very first visit, and in itself, this positive attitude was unique in comparison with their dealings with other doctors: it allowed them to have hope as well. My hope for these essays is that, despite their criticism of our society, they convey my ongoing optimism for the individual child.

Afterword

The rich diversity of cultures created by humankind is a testament to our ability to develop and adapt in diverse ways. But however varied different cultures may be, children are not endlessly malleable; they all share basic psychological and physical needs that must be met to ensure healthy development. The Childhood In America series examines the extent to which American culture meets children's irreducible needs. Without question, many children growing up in the United States lead privileged lives. They have been spared the ravages of war, poverty, malnourishment, sexism, and racism. However, despite our nation's resources, not all children share these privileges. Additionally, values that are central to American culture, such as self-reliance, individualism, privacy of family life, and consumerism, have created a climate in which parenting has become intolerably labor-intensive, and children are being taxed beyond their capacity for healthy adaptation. Record levels of psychiatric disturbance, violence, poverty, apathy, and despair among our children speak to our current cultural crisis.

Although our elected officials profess their commitment to "family values," policies that support family life are woefully lacking as well as inferior to those in other industrialized nations. American families are burdened by inadequate parental leave, a health care system that does not provide universal coverage for children, a minimum wage that is not a living wage, "welfare to work" policies that require parents to leave their children for long stretches of time, unregulated and inadequately subsidized day care, an unregulated entertainment industry that exposes children to sex and violence, and a two-tiered public education system that delivers inferior education to poor children and frequently ignores individual differences in learning styles and profiles of intelligence. As a result, many families are taxed to the breaking point. In addition, our fascination with technological innovation is creating a family lifestyle that is dominated by screens rather than human interaction.

The Childhood In America series seeks out leading childhood experts from across the disciplines to promote dialogue, research, and understanding regarding how best to raise and educate psychologically healthy children, to ensure that they will acquire the wisdom, heart, and courage needed to make choices for the betterment of society.

Sharna Olfman, PhD
Series Editor
Childhood in America

Notes

CHAPTER 1

1. UN International Narcotics Control Board. (2000). *Report of the UN International Narcotics Control Board.* New York: UN Publications.

2. Maier, T. (1998). *Dr. Spock: An American Life.* New York: Harcourt, Brace.

3. American Psychiatric Association. (1980). *Diagnostic and Statistical Manual of Mental Disorders* (3rd ed.). Washington, DC: American Psychiatric Association.

4. American Psychiatric Association. (1994). *Diagnostic and Statistical Manual of Mental Disorders* (4th ed.). Washington, DC: American Psychiatric Association.

5. Chess, S., et al. (1968). *Temperament and Behavior Disorders in Children.* New York: New York University Press.

6. Healy, D. (1996). *The Psychopharmacologists.* London: Altman.

7. Prozac was initially developed as an antianxiety agent. The marketing department at Eli Lilly, the makers of Prozac, instructed the researchers to shift the focus of treatment with Prozac from anxiety to depression. The pharmaceutical industry in the late 1980s was still reeling from a series of successful lawsuits against the makers of Valium-type drugs. It was believed that anything remotely associated with treating anxiety would be associated with the antidrug backlash involved with the Valium suits.

8. Healy, D. (1997). *The Antidepressant Era.* Boston: Harvard University Press.

9. Kramer, P. K. (1993). *Listening to Prozac.* New York: Viking Penguin.

10. Pam, A. (1995). "Biological psychiatry: science or pseudoscience." In *Pseudoscience in Biological Psychiatry,* ed. C. A. Ross and A. Pam. New York: John Wiley.

11. Ludwig, J. (2005). *Does Head Start Improve Children's Life Chances?* Madison, WI: Institute for Research on Poverty.

12. Angell, M. (2004). *The Truth about the Drug Companies.* New York: Random House.

13. Hechtman, L. (ed.). (1996). *Do They Grow Out of It? Long-Term Outcomes of Childhood Disorders.* Washington, DC: American Psychiatric Press.

14. Swanson, J. M., et al. (1993). Effects of stimulant medication on children with attention deficit disorder: A "review of reviews." *Exceptional Children*, 60, 154–161.

15. The campaign to improve housing and sanitation in the early twentieth-century, the introduction of childhood vaccinations in the mid-century, and the anti-smoking campaign of the last fifty years are some of the important exceptions to American medicine's general lack of interest in public health.

16. Schwartz, J. M., et al. (1996) Systematic changes in cerebral glucose metabolic rate after successful behavior modification treatment of obsessive-compulsive disorder. *Archives of General Psychiatry*, 54, 109–113.

17. Laing, R. D. (1965). *The Divided Self.* London: Penguin.

18. Greene, R. W. (1998). *The Explosive Child.* New York: Harper Collins.

19. Papolos, D., et al. (1999). *The Bipolar Child.* New York: Broadway Books.

20. Kranowitz, C. S. (2005). *The Out-of-Sync Child.* New York: Perigee Trade.

21. Rapoport, J. L., et al. (1980). Dextroamphetamine: Its cognitive and behavioral effects in normal and hyperactive boys and normal men. *Archives of General Psychiatry*, 37, 933–943.

22. Biederman, J., et al. (1992). Further evidence for family-genetic risk factors in attention deficit hyperactivity disorder: Patterns of comorbidity in probands and relatives in psychiatrically and pediatrically referred samples. *Archives of General Psychiatry*, 49, 728–738.

23. Barkley, R. A. (1997). *ADHD and the Nature of Self-Control.* New York: Guilford Press.

24. Biederman, J. (1998, November 15). Statement on *CBS Sunday Morning*.

25. Angell, M. (2004). *The Truth about the Drug Companies.* New York: Random House.

26. Stubbe, D. E., et al. (2002). A survey of early-career child and adolescent psychiatrists: Professional activities and perceptions. *Journal of the American Academy of Child and Adolescent Psychiatry*, 41, 123–130.

CHAPTER 2

1. This estimate is based on approximately 4–5 percent of children taking any kind of prescription stimulant in America. The estimate is derived from a number of studies and personal communications, including the following: Centers for Disease Control. (2005). Mental health in the United States: Prevalence of diagnosis and medication treatment for attention-deficit/hyperactivity disorder—United States, 2003. *MMWR Weekly*, 54, 842–847; Harris, G. (2005, September 15). Use of attention-deficit drugs is found to soar among adults. *New York Times*, A14; Cuffe, S. P., et al. (2005). Prevalence and correlates of ADHD symptoms in the National Health Interview Survey. *Journal of Attention Disorders*, 9, 392–401; Cox, E. R., et al. (2003). Geographic variation in the prevalence of stimulant medication use among children 5 to 14 years old: Results from a commercially insured US sample. *Pediatrics*, 111, 237–243; Personal communication with Julie Zito, PhD, University of Maryland School of Pharmacy, Baltimore, MD.

2. Harris, G., (2005, September 15). Use of attention-deficit drugs is found to soar among adults. *New York Times*, A14; Faraone, S. V., and J. Biederman (2005).

What is the prevalence of adult ADHD? Results of a population screen of 966 adults. *Journal of Attention Disorders, 9,* 384–391.

3. Methylphenidate Annual Production Quota (1990–2005). (2005). Washington, DC: Office of Public Affairs, Drug Enforcement Administration, Department of Justice.

4. Amphetamine Annual Production Quota (1990–2005). (2005). Washington, DC: Office of Public Affairs, Drug Enforcement Administration, Department of Justice.

5. UN International Narcotics Control Board. (2000). *Report of the UN International Narcotics Control Board.* New York: UN Publications.

6. Christakis, D. A., et al. (2004). Early television exposure and subsequent attentional problems in children. *Pediatrics, 113,* 708–713.

7. UN International Narcotics Control Board. (2000). *Report of the UN International Narcotics Control Board.* New York: UN Publications.

8. Angell M. (2004). *The Truth about the Drug Companies.* New York: Random House.

9. International Narcotics Control Act of 1972.

10. Myers, D. G. (2000). *The American Paradox: Spiritual Hunger in an Age of Plenty.* New Haven, CT: Yale University Press.

CHAPTER 3

1. Faraone, S. V., et al. (2003). The worldwide prevalence of ADHD: Is it an American condition? *World Psychiatry, 2,* 104–113.

2. Harris, G. (2005, September 15). Use of attention-deficit drugs is found to soar among adults. *New York Times,* A14.

3. Swanson, J. M., et al. (1993). Effects of stimulant medication on children with attention deficit disorder: A "review of reviews." *Exceptional Children, 60,* 154–161.

4. Gaub, M., et al. (1997). Gender differences in ADHD: A meta-analysis and critical review. *Journal of the American Academy of Child and Adolescent Psychiatry, 36,* 1036–1045.

5. Harris, G. (2005). *See* note 2.

6. Biederman, J., et al. (2002). Influence of gender on attention deficit hyperactivity disorder in children referred to a psychiatric clinic. *American Journal of Psychiatry, 159,* 36–42.

7. Biederman, J., et al. (2002). *See* note 6.

8. Nadeau, K. G., et al. (eds.). (2002). *Understanding Women with ADHD.* Silver Spring, MD: Advantage Books.

9. Quinn, P., et al. (2004). Perceptions of girls and ADHD: Results from a national survey. *Medscape General Medicine, 6,* 2–13.

10. Biederman, J., et al. (2005). Absence of gender effects on attention deficit hyperactivity disorder: Findings in nonreferred subjects. *American Journal of Psychiatry, 162,* 1083–1089.

11. Quinn, P. O. (2005). Treating adolescent girls and women with ADHD: Gender-specific issues. *JCLP/In Session, 61,* 579–587.

12. Brown, G. W. (1978). *Social Origins of Depression: A Study of Psychiatric Disorder in Women.* London: Tavistock.

CHAPTER 4

1. American Academy of Pediatrics. (2000). Clinical practice guideline: Diagnosis and evaluation of the child with attention-deficit/hyperactivity disorder. *Pediatrics*, 105, 1158–1170; American Academy of Pediatrics. (2001). Clinical practice guideline: Treatment of the school-aged child with attention-deficit/hyperactivity disorder. *Pediatrics*, 108, 1033–1044.

2. Greenhill, L. L., et al. (2002). Practice parameter for the use of stimulant medications in the treatment of children, adolescents, and adults. *Journal of the American Academy of Child Adolescent Psychiatry*, 41, 26S–49S.

3. Krain, A. L., et al. (2005). The role of treatment acceptability in the initiation of treatment for ADHD. *Journal of Attention Disorders*, 9, 425–434.

4. Rappley, M. D. (2005). Attention-deficit/hyperactivity disorder. *New England Journal of Medicine*, 352, 165–173.

5. Pelham, W. E., et al. (1998). Empirically supported psychosocial treatments for attention-deficit hyperactivity disorder. *Journal of Clinical Child Psychology*, 27, 190–205; Pelham, W. E., et al. (2005). Implementation of a comprehensive school-wide behavioral intervention. *Journal of Attention Disorders*, 9, 248–260; Maughan, D. R., et al. (2005). Behavioral parent training as a treatment for externalizing behavior disorders: A meta-analysis. *School Psychology Review*, 34, 267–286.

6. Evans, S. W., et al. (2005). Development of a school-based treatment program for middle school youth with ADHD. *Journal of Attention Disorders*, 9, 333–342; Semrud-Clikeman, M., et al. (1999). An intervention approach for children with teacher-and parent-identified attentional difficulties. *Journal of Learning Disabilities*, 32, 581–590; Tutty, S., et al. (2003). Enhancing behavioral and social skill functioning in children newly diagnosed with ADHD in a pediatric setting. *Journal of Developmental Behavioral Pediatrics*, 24, 51–57.

7. Special Section: ADHD, comorbidity and treatment outcomes in the MTA study. (2001). *Journal of the American Academy of Child and Adolescent Psychiatry*, 40, 134–196.

8. Klein, R. G., et al. (2004). Design and rationale of control study of long-term methylphenidate and multi-modal psychosocial treatment in children with ADHD. *Journal of the American Academy of Child and Adolescent Psychiatry*, 43, 782–801; Klein, R. G., et al. (2004). Symptomatic improvement in children with ADHD treated with long-term methylphenidate and multi-modal psychosocial treatment. *Journal of the American Academy of Child and Adolescent Psychiatry*, 43, 802–811.

9. Conners, C. K., et al. (2001). Multimodal treatment of ADHD in the MTA: An alternative outcome analysis. *Journal of the American Academy of Child and Adolescent Psychiatry*, 40, 159–167.

10. Ibid.

11. MTA Cooperative Group. (2004). National Institute of Mental Health multimodal treatment study of ADHD follow-up: Changes in effectiveness and growth after treatment. *Pediatrics*, 113, 762–770.

12. Handler, M. W., et al. (2005). Assessment of ADHD: Differences across psychology specialty areas. *Journal of Attention Disorders*, 9, 402–412.

13. Jensen, P. S., et al. (1999). Are stimulants over-prescribed? Treatment of ADHD in four U.S. communities. *Journal of the American Academy of Child and Adolescent Psychiatry*, 38, 797–804.

14. Center for Disease Control. (2005). Morbidity and Mortality Weekly Report, 54(34), http://www.cdc.gov/mmwr; Medco Health Solutions. (2005). ADHD medication use growing faster among adults than children. New Research. http://www.medco.com

15. Bussing, R., et al. (1998). Children in special education programs: ADHD and use of services and unmet needs. *American Journal of Public Health*, 88, 880–886.

16. Barbaresi, W. J., et al. (2002). How common is ADHD? *Archives of Pediatric and Adolescent Medicine*, 156, 217–224.

17. Angold, A., et al. (2000). Stimulant treatment for children: A community perspective. *Journal of the American Academy of Child and Adolescent Psychiatry*, 39, 975–984.

18. Chako, A., et al. (2005). Stimulant medication effects in a summer treatment program among young children with attention-deficit hyperactivity disorder. *Journal of the American Academy of Child and Adolescent Psychiatry*, 44, 249–257.

19. Chako, A., et al. (2005). *See* note 18.

20. Sawyer, M. G., et al. (2004). Relationship between parents' perceptions of children's need for professional help. *Journal of the American Academy of Child and Adolescent Psychiatry*, 43, 1355–1363.

21. Gordon, M., et al. (2006). Symptoms versus impairment: The case for respecting DSM-IV's Criterion D. *Journal of Attention Disorders*, 9, 465–475.

22. Goldstein, S., et al. (eds.). (2002). *Clinician's Guide to Adult ADHD: Assessment and Intervention*. New York: Academic Press.

23. Connor, D. F., et al. (2002). Psychopharmacology and aggression. I: Meta-analysis of stimulant effects on overt/covert aggression related behaviors in ADHD. *Journal of the American Academy of Child and Adolescent Psychiatry*, 41, 253–261; Faraone, S. V., et al. (2004). Meta-analysis of the efficacy of methylphenidate for treating adult attention deficit hyperactivity disorder. *Journal of Clinical Psychopharmacology*, 24, 24–29.

24. Deater-Deckard, K., et al. (2004). Resilience in gene-environment transactions. In *Handbook of Resilience In Children*, ed. S. Goldstein and R. Brooks. New York: Kluwer/Academic Press.

25. Strayhorn, J. M. (2002). Self-control: Theory and research. *Journal of the American Academy of Child and Adolescent Psychiatry*, 41, 7–27; Strayhorn, J. M. (2002). Self-control: Toward systematic training programs. *Journal of the American Academy of Child and Adolescent Psychiatry*, 41, 17–27.

CHAPTER 5

1. I spoke with Dr. Camara first in May and then again in November of 2005.

2. College Board. (2005, August 30). SAT math scores for 2005 highest on record. *College Board Press Release*.

3. All the ETS research on the SAT and accommodations was done when the highest score possible was 1600. Since 2005, a new version of the test allows for a highest score of 2400.

4. Director of Admissions Office, University of California, Berkeley, September 2005.

5. College Board. (2000, January). Research Notes: Testing with extended time on the SAT I: Effects for students with learning disabilities. Office of Research and Development. RN-08.

6. Mandinach, E. B., et al. (2002). The impact of flagging on the admission process: Policies, practices and implications. New York: College Board Research Report No. 2002-2.

7. Cox, E. R., et al. (2003). Geographic variation in the prevalence of stimulant medication use among children 5 to 14 years old: Results from a commercially insured U.S. sample. *Pediatrics*, 111, 237–243.

8. Diller, L. H. (1998). *Running on Ritalin*. New York: Bantam.

9. Mandinach, E. B., et al. (2002). The impact of flagging on the admission process: Policies, practices and implications. New York: College Board Research Report No. 2002-2.

10. Mandinach, E. B., et al. (2002). *See* note 9.

11. College Board. (2000, January). *See* note 5.

12. Nonstandard Designation Removal: The college board and disabilities rights advocates announce agreement to drop flagging from standardized tests. (2003). http://www.collegeboard.com/disable/students/html/ndr.html

13. College Board. (2005). *College-Bound Seniors: Total Group Profile Report.*

14. Personal communication. (2005, December). Telephone interview with Eric Myers.

15. Ball, H. (2000). *The Bakke Case: Race, Education, and Affirmative Action.* Lawrence: University Press of Kansas.

16. Rojewski, J. W. (1999). Occupational and educational aspirations and attainment of young adults with and without LD 2 years after high school completion. *Journal of Learning Disabilities*, 32, 533–552.

17. Kadison, R. (2005). Getting an edge: Use of stimulants and antidepressants in college. *New England Journal of Medicine*, 353, 1089–1091.

CHAPTER 6

1. Zernike, K., et al. (2001, August 19). Schools' backing of behavior drugs comes under fire. *New York Times*, 1+.

2. Methylphenidate Annual Production Quota (1990–2005). (2005). Washington, DC: Office of Public Affairs, Drug Enforcement Administration, Department of Justice.

3. UN International Narcotics Control Board (2000). *Report of the UN International Narcotics Control Board.* New York: UN Publications.

4. Section 25 of the Individuals with Disabilities Education Improvement Act (IDEA) signed into law on December 3, 2004. http://www.nectas.unc. edu/idea/Idea2004.asp

5. The U.S. House of Representatives passed an amendment in the session ending 2005 that extended the breadth of coverage against forced medication to include all psychiatric drugs for all public school students. The amendment awaits Senate action in the next session of Congress.

6. Barlas, S. (2005, March 1). Mental health screening controversy continues. *Psychiatric Times*, 74.

7. Kessler, R. C., et al. (2005). Lifetime prevalence and age-of-onset distributions of DSM-IV disorders in the National Comorbidity Survey Replication. *Archives of General Psychiatry*, 62, 593–602.

8. Horwitz, A. V., et al. (Winter 2006). The epidemic in mental illness: Clinical fact or survey artifact? *Contexts*, 19–23.

CHAPTER 7

1. Hartson, J. N. (2005, December 13). Letters to the Editor. *The ADHD Report*, 15–16.

2. Hartson, J. N. (2005, December 13). *See* note 1.

3. Parens, E. (1998). Is better always good? *Hastings Center Report*, Special Supplement (Jan–Feb), S1–S17.

4. In "For Preventing The Children of Poor People in Ireland from Being a Burden to Their Parents or Country, and for Making Them Beneficial to the Public," Jonathan Swift suggested ironically that a "young healthy child" of "a year old" would have made "a most delicious, nourishing, and wholesome food, whether stewed, roasted, baked, or boiled."

CHAPTER 8

1. This estimate is based on approximately 4–5 percent of children taking any kind of prescription stimulant in America. The estimate is derived from a number of studies and personal communications, including the following: Centers for Disease Control. (2005). Mental health in the United States: Prevalence of diagnosis and medication treatment for attention-deficit/hyperactivity disorder—United States, 2003. *MMWR Weekly*, 54, 842–847; Harris, G. (2005, September 15). Use of attention-deficit drugs is found to soar among adults. *New York Times*, A14; Cuffe, S. P., et al. (2005). Prevalence and correlates of ADHD symptoms in the National Health Interview Survey. *Journal of Attention Disorders*, 9, 392–401; Cox, E. R., et al. (2003). Geographic variation in the prevalence of stimulant medication use among children 5 to 14 years old: Results from a commercially insured US sample. *Pediatrics*, 111, 237–243; Personal communication with Julie Zito, PhD, University of Maryland School of Pharmacy, Baltimore, MD.

2. Diller, L. H. (1998). *Running on Ritalin*. New York: Bantam.

3. Bradley, C. (1937). The behavior of children receiving Benzedrine. *American Journal of Psychiatry*, 94, 577–585.

4. Weiss, B., et al. (1962). The enhancement of human performance by caffeine and the amphetamines. *Pharmacological Review*, 14, 1–36.

5. Rapoport, J. L. et al. (1980). Dextroamphetamine: Its cognitive and behavioral effects in normal and hyperactive boys and normal men. *Archives of General Psychiatry*, 37, 933–943.

6. Kadison, R. (2005). Getting an edge: Use of stimulants and antidepressants in college. *New England Journal of Medicine*, 353, 1089–1091.

7. McCabe, S. E., et al. (2005). Non-medical use of prescription stimulants among U.S. college students: Prevalence and correlates from a national survey. *Addiction*, 99, 96–106.

8. Kroutil, L. A., et al. (2006, February 7). Nonmedical use of prescription stimulants in the United States. *Drug and Alcohol Dependence*, in press and online at http://www.ncbi.nlm.nih.gov/entrez/query.fcgi?cmd=Retrieve&db=pubmed&dopt=Abstract&list_uids=16480836&query_hl=1&itool=pubmed_docsum

9. Methylphenidate Annual Production Quota (1990–2005). (2005). Washington, DC: Office of Public Affairs, Drug Enforcement Administration, Department of Justice.

10. Colman, E. (2005, September 6). Anorectics on trial: A half century of federal regulation of prescription appetite suppressants. *Annals of Internal Medicine*, 143, 380–385.

11. UN International Narcotics Control Board. (1999, February 23). *Report of the UN International Narcotics Control Board, No. 4*. New York: UN Publications.

12. Yellen, B. (1970). Doing something about amphetamines. *New England Journal of Medicine*, 10, 1349–1350; U.S. Senate Committee on the Judiciary, Subcommittee to Investigate Juvenile Delinquency. (1972). *Amphetamine legislation 1971*. Hearings, Ninety-second Congress. Washington, DC: U.S. Government Printing Office.

CHAPTER 9

1. Selvini Palazzoli, M., et al. (1978). *Paradox and Counterparadox: A New Model in the Therapy of the Family in Schizophrenic Transaction*, trans. Elisabeth V. Burt. New York: Jason Aronson.

2. Selvini Palazzoli, M., et al. (1989). *Family Games: General Models of Psychotic Processes in the Family*, trans. Veronica Kleiber. New York: W.W. Norton.

3. Haley, J. (1980). *Leaving Home: The Therapy of Disturbed Young People*. New York: McGraw-Hill.

4. Hulbert, A. (2003). *Raising America: Experts, Parents, and a Century of Advice about Children*. New York: Alfred Knopf.

5. Thienemann, M., et al. (2006). A parent-only group intervention for children with anxiety disorders: Pilot study. *Journal of the American Academy of Child and Adolescent Psychiatry*, 45, 37–46; Bogels, S. M., et al. (2006). Family cognitive behavioral therapy for children and adolescents with clinical anxiety disorders. *Journal of the American Academy of Child and Adolescent Psychiatry*, 45, 134–141.

6. White, M., et al. (1990). *Narrative means to therapeutic ends*. New York: Norton.

7. March, J., et al. (1998). *OCD in Children and Adolescents: A Cognitive-Behavioral Treatment Manual*. New York: Guilford Press.

CHAPTER 10

1. Telephone conversations in November 2005 with Russell Barkley.

2. Barkley, R. (1990). *Attention-Deficit Hyperactivity Disorder: A Handbook for Diagnosis and Treatment*. New York: Guilford Press.

3. Barkley, R. (1997). *ADHD and the Nature of Self-Control*. New York: Guilford Press.

CHAPTER 11

1. Surowiecki, J. (2001, January 15). What price Hollywood? *The New Yorker*, 76, 38.

2. Pliska, S. R., et al. (2006). The Texas children's medication algorithm project: revision of the algorithm for pharmacotherapy of attention-deficit/hyperactivity disorder. *Journal of the American Academy of Child and Adolescent Psychiatry*, 45, 642–657.

3. Zoler, M. L. (2004, November). ADHD comparison favors methylphenidate. *Clinical Psychiatry News*, 32, 33.

4. *FDA Consumer* (March–April 2005). New warning about ADHD drug, 39, 3.

5. Miller, M. C. (2005). What is the significance of the new warnings about suicide risk with Strattera? *Harvard Mental Health Letter*, 22, 8.

6. Harris, G. (2005, September 15). Use of attention-deficit drugs is found to soar among adults. *New York Times*, p. A14.

CHAPTER 12

1. Sobel, D. (1999). *Galileo's Daughter: A Historical Memoir of Science, Faith, and Love*. New York: Walker & Co.

2. Lambert, N. M., et al. (1998). Prospective study of tobacco smoking and substance dependencies among samples of ADHD and non-ADHD participants. *Journal of Learning Disorders*, 31, 533–544.

3. Biederman, J., et al. (1999). Pharmacotherapy of attention-deficit/hyperactivity disorder reduces risk for substance use disorder. *Pediatrics*, 104, e20.

4. Wilens, T. E., et al. (2003). Does stimulant therapy of attention-deficit/hyperactivity disorder beget later substance abuse? A meta-analytic review of the literature. *Pediatrics*, 111, 179–185.

5. Noble, J. H. (2006). Meta-analysis: Methods, strengths, weaknesses and political uses. *Journal of Laboratory and Clinical Medicine*, 147, 7–20.

6. Barkley R. A., et al. (2003). Does the treatment of attention-deficit/hyperactivity disorder with stimulants contribute to drug use/abuse? A 13-year prospective study. *Pediatrics*, 111, 97–109.

7. Cox, E. R., et al. (2003). Geographic variation in the prevalence of stimulant medication use among children 5 to 14 years old: Results from a commercially insured US sample. *Pediatrics*, 111, 237–243.

8. UN International Narcotics Control Board. (2000). *Report of the UN International Narcotics Control Board*. New York: UN Publications.

9. Bradley, C. (1937). The behavior of children receiving Benzedrine. *American Journal of Psychiatry*, 94, 577–585.

10. Rapoport, J. L., et al. (1980). Dextroamphetamine: Its cognitive and behavioral effects in normal and hyperactive boys and normal men. *Archives of General Psychiatry*, 37, 933–943.

11. MTA Cooperative Group. (1999). A 14-month randomized clinical trial of treatment strategies for ADHD. *Archives of General Psychiatry*, 56, 1073–1086.

12. Satterfield, J. H., et al. (1987). Therapeutic interventions to prevent delinquency in hyperactive boys. *Journal of the American Academy of Child and Adolescent Psychiatry*, 26, 56–64.

13. Schenk, S., et al. (1997). Sensitization and tolerance in psychostimulant self-administration. *Pharmacology, Biochemistry and Behavior*, 57, 543–550.

14. Volkow, N. D., et al. (1995). Is methylphenidate like cocaine? Studies on their pharmacokinetics and distribution in the human brain. *Archives in General Psychiatry*, 52, 456–463.

15. Strakowski, S. M., et al. (1998). Progressive behavioral response to repeated d-amphetamine challenge: Further evidence for sensitization in humans. *Biological Psychiatry*, 44, 1171–1177.

16. Barkley, R. A., et al. (2003). *See* note 6.

17. Angell, M. (2004). *The Truth about the Drug Companies*. New York: Random House.

18. Angell, M. (2000). Is academic medicine for sale? *New England Journal of Medicine*, 342, 1516–1518.

19. Greenhill, L. L., et al. (eds.). (2000). *Ritalin: Theory and Practice*, 2nd ed. Larchmont, NY: M.A. Liebert Publishers.

20. DeFao, Janine. (2006, May 6). Obituary of Nadine Lambert, *San Francisco Chronicle*.

CHAPTER 13

1. Department of Health and Human Services, Food and Drug Administration, Center for Drug Evaluation and Research, Psychopharmacologic Drug and Advisory Committee with the Pediatric Subcommittee of the Anti-Infective Drugs Advisory Committee. (2004, February 2); Department of Health and Human Services, Food and Drug Administration, Psychopharmacologic Drugs Advisory Committee. (2004). Joint meeting with the Pediatric Advisory Committee, September 13–14.

2. Healy, D. (2004). *Let Them Eat Prozac: The Unhealthy Relationship between the Pharmaceutical Industry and Depression*. New York: New York University Press.

3. Healy, D. (2003). Lines of evidence on the risks of suicide with selective serotonin reuptake inhibitors. *Psychotherapy Psychosomatics*, 72, 71–79.

4. *Best Pharmaceuticals for Children Act of 2002*, Pub L No. 107–109.

5. Goode, E. (2003, December 11). British warning on antidepressant use for youth. *New York Times*, p. 1+.

6. Stubbe, D. E., et al. (2002). A survey of early-career child and adolescent psychiatrists: Professional activities and perceptions. *Journal of the American Academy of Child and Adolescent Psychiatry*, 41, 123–130.

7. Diller, L. (2004, March 24). Keeping doctors in the dark. *Washington Post*, p. A21.

8. Leslie, L. K., et al. (2005). The Food and Drug Administration's deliberations on antidepressant use in pediatric patients. *Pediatrics*, 166, 195–204.

9. Brennan, T. A., et al. (2006). Health industry practices that create conflicts of interest: A policy proposal for academic medical centers. *Journal of the American Medical Association*, 295, 429–433.

10. Berndt, E. R. (2005). To inform or persuade? Direct-to-consumer advertising of prescription drugs. *New England Journal of Medicine*, 352, 325–328.

CHAPTER 14

1. Office of Special Education and Rehabilitative Services, Department of Education. (1991). Memorandum. Section C: Clarification of policy to address the needs of children with attention deficit disorders within general and/or special education. Washington, DC: Office of Special Education and Rehabilitative Services, Department of Education.

2. American Psychiatric Association. (1980). *Diagnostic and Statistical Manual of Mental Disorders* (3rd ed.). Washington, DC: American Psychiatric Association.

3. Methylphenidate Annual Production Quota (1990–2005). (2005). Washington, DC: Office of Public Affairs, Drug Enforcement Administration, Department of Justice.

4. Zernike, K., et al. (2001, August 19). Schools' backing of behavior drugs comes under fire. *New York Times*, 1+.

5. Section 25 of the Individuals with Disabilities Education Improvement Act (IDEA), signed into law on December 3, 2004. http://www.nectas.unc.edu/idea/Idea2004.asp

6. Angell, M. (2004). *The Truth about the Drug Companies.* New York: Random House.

7. Furedi, F. (2004). *Therapy Culture: Cultivating Vulnerability in an Uncertain Age.* London: Routledge.

8. Myers, D. G. (2000). *The American Paradox: Spiritual Hunger in an Age of Plenty.* New Haven, CT: Yale University Press.

9. Myers, D. G. (2000). *See* note 8.

10. Borger, C., et al. (2006). Health Spending Projections through 2015: Changes on the Horizon. *Health Affairs*, 10.1377/hlthaff.25.w61.

11. Costello, E. J., et al. (2003). Relationships between poverty and psychopathology: A natural experiment. *Journal of the American Medical Association*, 290, 2023–2029.

12. Horwitz, A. V. (2002). *Creating Mental Illness.* Chicago: University of Chicago Press.

13. Lollar, D. J., et al. (2005). Diagnosis to Function: Classification for Children and Youths. *Journal of Developmental & Behavioral Pediatrics*, 26, 323–330.

PROFESSIONAL AND FAMILY FACTORS: A PERSONAL POSTSCRIPT

1. Carter, S., et al. (1974). *Neurology of Infancy and Childhood.* New York: Appleton-Century-Crofts.

2. Bateson, G. (1987). *Steps to an Ecology of Mind: Collected Essays in Anthropology, Psychiatry, Evolution, and Epistemology.* Northvale, NJ: Aronson.

3. Chess, S., et al. (1986). *Temperament in Clinical Practice.* New York: Guilford Press.

4. Brazelton, T. B. (1969). *Infants and Mothers: Differences in Development.* New York: Delacorte Press.

5. American Psychiatric Association. (1980). *Diagnostic and Statistical Manual of Mental Disorders* (3rd ed.). Washington, DC: American Psychiatric Association.

6. Engel, G. L. (1977). The need for a new medical model: A challenge for biomedicine. *Science*, 196, 129–135.

Index

About the Author, Series Editor, and Advisers

AUTHOR

LAWRENCE H. DILLER, MD, practices the specialty of behavioral/developmental pediatrics in Walnut Creek, California. He attended the College of Physicians and Surgeons, Columbia University, and trained at the renowned Child Study Unit of the University of California, San Francisco, as well as at the Mental Research Institute of Palo Alto. He has authored two earlier books, *Running on Ritalin: A Physician Reflects on Children, Society, and Performance in a Pill* (1998), and *Should I Medicate My Child? Sane Solutions for Troubled Kids with—and without— Medication* (2002), in addition to numerous articles for the lay and professional press. Dr. Diller has appeared on television, radio and in the print media many times. In 2000 he won the Public Affairs award from the Society for Professional Journalism. He testified as an expert on Ritalin before a U.S. Congressional subcommittee in 2000 and for the President's council on Bioethics in 2002. He and his wife of thirty-three years have two teenage sons. His website can be found at www.docdiller.com.

SERIES EDITOR

SHARNA OLFMAN, PhD, is a clinical psychologist and associate professor of psychology in the Department of Humanities at Point Park University, Pittsburgh, where she teaches child development and directs the Childhood and Society Symposium series. Dr. Olfman edited and contributed to the following books: *All Work and No Play. . . : How Educational Reforms Are Harming Our Preschoolers* (Praeger, 2004) and *Childhood Lost: How American Culture Is Failing Our Kids* (Praeger, 2005). Dr. Olfman has published and presented papers on gender development, infant care and child psychopathology, and women's mental health.

SERIES ADVISERS

JOAN ALMON is coordinator of the U.S. branch of the Alliance for Childhood and cochair of the Waldorf Early Childhood Association of North America. She is internationally renowned as a consultant to Waldorf educators and training programs, and she is the author of numerous articles on Waldorf education.

JANE M. HEALY has appeared on most major media in the United States and is frequently consulted regarding the effects of new technologies on the developing brain. She holds a PhD in educational psychology from Case Western University and has done postdoctoral work in developmental neuropsychology. Formerly on the faculties of Cleveland State University and John Carroll University, she is internationally recognized as a lecturer and a consultant with many years' experience as a classroom teacher, reading/learning specialist, and elementary administrator. She is the author of numerous articles, as well as the books *Endangered Minds: Why Our Children Don't Think and What We Can Do about It* (1999), *How to Have an Intelligent and Creative Conversation with Your Kids* (1994), *Your Child's Growing Mind: A Guide to Learning and Brain Development from Birth to Adolescence* (1994), and *Failure to Connect: How Computers Affect Our Children's Minds—For Better and Worse* (1998).

STUART SHANKER, PhD Oxon, is a distinguished professor of philosophy and psychology at York University in Toronto. He is, with Stanley Greenspan, codirector of the Council of Human Development and associate chair for Canada in the Interdisciplinary Council of Learning and Developmental Disorders. He has won numerous awards and currently holds grants from the Unicorn Foundation, the Templeton Foundation, and Cure Autism Now. His books include *The First Idea: How Symbols, Language, and Intelligence Evolved from Our Primate Ancestors to Modern Humans* (2004), *Toward a Psychology of Global Interdependency: A Framework for International Collaboration* (2002), and *Wittgenstein's Remarks on the Foundations of Animal Intelligence* (1998).

MEREDITH F. SMALL, PhD, is a writer and professor of anthropology at Cornell University. Trained as a primate behaviorist, she now writes about all areas of anthropology, natural history, and health. Besides numerous publications in academic journals, Dr. Small contributes regularly to *Discover* and *New Scientist*, and she is a commentator on National Public Radio's "All Things Considered." She is the author of five books, including *What's Love Got to Do with It? The Evolution of Human Mating* (1996), *Our Babies, Ourselves: How Biology and Culture Shape the Way We Parent* (1999), and *Kids: How Biology and Culture Shape the Way We Parent* (2001, paperback 2002). Dr. Small is currently working on a book about the anthropology of mental health titled *The Culture of Our Discontent*, in which she explores the now-standard medical model of mental illness with the causes and cures of "abnormal" behavior in traditional cultures.